The Cabin on Sawmill Creek
A Western *Walden*

The Cabin on Sawmill Creek
A Western *Walden*

Mary Jo Churchwell

The CAXTON PRINTERS, Ltd.
Caldwell, Idaho
1997

Library of Congress Cataloging-in-Publication Data

Churchwell, Mary Jo, 1942 –
  The Cabin on Sawmill Creek: a Western Walden / Mary Jo
Churchwell
        p. cm.
    ISBN 0-87004-380-3   (pbk.)
    1. Churchwell, Mary Jo. 1942- . 2. Challis Region (Idaho)--
Biography. 3. Salmon River (Idaho)--Biography. 4. Challis
Region (Idaho) -- Social life and customs. 5. Salmon River
(Idaho)--Social life and customs. 6. Frontier and pioneer life-
-Idaho--Challis Region. 7. Frontier and pioneer life--Idaho--
Salmon River.
I. Title.
F754.C5C48   1997
979.6'72033'092--dc21
[b]   97-20584
                                                                        CIP

Lithographed and bound in the United States of America by
The Caxton Printers, Ltd.
Caldwell, Idaho
162405
C.W.C.

Dedication

For my mother, Mary Paradise Stephens.

Table of Contents

Illustrations

All photos by Mary Jo Churchwell.

INTRODUCTION

*A man dwells in his native valley like a corolla
in its calyx, like an acorn in its cup. Here, of course,
is all that you love, all that you expect, all that you
are . . . . Here is all the best and all the worst you
can imagine. What more do you want?*
–Henry David Thoreau

In central Idaho, the ranges of the Rockies bunch on their
march through the state, making access so difficult
development isn't even thought of yet. This is wilderness –
not pristine wilderness like the fur trappers knew, not
wilderness by Alaskan standards – but wilderness
nonetheless. It is the limit of the habitable earth, still
uncivilized some would say.

In this mountain vastness, among the ragged peaks of
the Sawtooth Range, the Salmon River rises in a trickle of
snowmelt and begins its undammed route to the Snake.
The Salmon meanders through meadows of its own making. It divides and forms islands of sand where geese raise
their young. It curves and creates cattail marshes where
deer come to drink, blackbirds to breed, and ducks to winter warm beside the thermal springs. Where the river boils
backwards, helmeted river-runners ride. Where it slows to
riffles, anglers stand in rubber boots, throwing lines across
the backs of migrating steelhead. Where the river carved a
valley, at the far end of the rainbow, the town of Challis
lies, a classic picture of the old Wild West.

The curves in the Salmon River (known locally as the
"River") account for the curves on Scenic Byway 93 (known
locally as the "Highway"). This ribbon of pavement con-

nects Challis with rural-route ranches and one-lane dirt roads that follow feeder creeks down from the peaks of the Salmon River Range. These roads bear numbers not names. They drift closed in winter, wash out in spring. Ten miles north of Challis, where the river meets Morgan Creek, such a road begins its climb to the top. The road runs wide through wild pastures. Then it narrows where the cliffs close in. Where cottonwoods give way to aspens and the road crosses a creeklet called Sawmill, the two ruts we call a driveway begin.

Our driveway runs for a mile, through acres of wildflowers in some seasons or acres of snow, crossing the creek twice without benefit of bridges. Within that mile it passes through a gate separating hundreds of miles of public pasture from two parcels of private pasture. Finally the driveway passes through our gate and up the sagebrushed hillside where it dead ends at our back door.

Thirteen years ago Stew and I came into Salmon River country, not to hide out for a few summers but to live year-round in sync with the seasons. Having left our life in smoggy Southern California, having left the tameness and sameness of our days and a future that offered little of what we wanted, we came to live off the land (as they used to say it). Here in Sawmill Canyon, far removed from humankind, we chipped out a niche and found our way back to a better time.

Lucky us. There is no time but right now, no place but right here. From our porch, national forest lands heave and hump in every direction to all horizons near and far. We are surrounded by peaks pointed and packed with snow until late June. When I stand in my garden, in the warm summer sunshine, with the green grass growing all around, I know the only world worth living in is the world on Sawmill Creek.

The mountains control our lives. The climate brings

killing frost ten months a year and locks us in from November to May. But the climate only partly defines our lifestyle, a lifestyle Spartan to be sure but bare-boned by no means. To say we are poor isn't exact. Ours isn't a millstone poverty, a poverty we haven't the strength or the means to lift off our backs. Ours is a voluntary poverty, something we don't exactly embrace but something we willingly accept as payment for riches beyond belief. We do not suffer, believe me. Like Thoreau we measure wealth not in money but in sunny hours and summer days, in the abundance and diversity of wildlife, in happiness and good health and air so clear you can see every pine needle. Our work is not bound by bosses but by nature's saner jurisdiction. Every day we deal with things that are real. As the seasons change from white to green to greener to gold, our labors turn to foraging, gardening, fishing, and hunting. In sum, we have fun. Like the folks in town say, "Those Churchwells don't work."

Every culture needs its dropouts. Call us countercultural pilgrims, if you will, because we scorn this high-tech age we live in. Call us old hippies (or whatever hippies are called nowadays) because we moan that we were born too late when so much that was good is gone. Bartering is gone. Now goods and services are paid for by check not moonshine or country hams. The Age of the Horse is gone. It has been dead and buried for decades. Driving a horse-drawn buckboard over these crooked mountain roads would be about as safe as driving it on the Hollywood Freeway at rush hour, and just as insane. Even more disheartening is that we old-fashioned meat hunters must abide by modern game laws, laws designed for trophy hunters, laws that run contrary to natural selection, and at times even common sense. But what is most disheartening of all is that today's burgeoning population has fueled the fires of environmental crisis. Where Sawmill's frontiersmen fought weather and wolves, Stew and I fight the managers of public lands, who all too often cater to the politics of the day. While dreaming of the way it was, we hope for the way it will be.

There are all kinds of costs nowadays having nothing to do with old-fashioned simple survival. There are taxes on property, goods, and gasoline. There are fees for license plates, for firewood collecting, for hunting and fishing. Needless to say, Stew and I have learned to live on a shoe-string budget. Give or take a few hundred bucks, $2,400 sees us through a year. This covers taxes, fees, liability insurance for the truck, replacement parts for the truck, building repairs for the house, propane, postage stamps, flour, beans, and all those other necessaries that are part of living off the land today.

This book tells how we straddle the past and the present, making the best of both worlds. It tells how we live luxuriously on a self-imposed budget. It tells how we built our log cabin with hand tools, how we garden organically in a heroic climate, how we hunt, fish, and forage for subsistence. It tells how we survive snowbound seclusion and how we survived home schooling our kids. Yes this book tells it all. Here's all the outrageous but true stuff you've ever wanted to know about living in the wilderness, a book packed with information, most of it accurate.

But this book is not just another homesteading how-to. It's way more than that. You see, in the same manner that our cabin on Sawmill Creek serves as a base camp for higher adventures, this book serves as an organizational device for portraying the central Idaho Rockies, the seasons, the landscape, the wildlife, the history, and one family's affairs, their simple joys and not so simple sorrows. If you have been here before, this book will take you back. If you haven't, it will bring you closer than you are ever likely to come.

1
Escape

I went to the woods because I wished to live deliberately, to front only the essential facts of life, and see if I could not learn what it had to teach, and not, when I came to die, discover that I had not lived.
—Henry David Thoreau

January 15: Cold patterns the windowpanes. It came in last night, from the north, on a wind that tore through the aspens, whooped at the door, and flailed the fiberglass roof of the greenhouse, keeping us awake, anxious, and alert. Now at dawn Sawmill Canyon is calm. Except for the brief howling bursts of two coyotes, ridge-top coyote and creek-bottom coyote calling up the sun like roosters, Sawmill Canyon is steeped in silence, not a looming desolate silence but a deep abiding peace.

The cabin, surrounded by silence, is silent as well, or silent enough anyway. Occasionally there's a thump in Chad's bedroom although there's no one in there. Both boys are gone, making their mark on society. And there are cheerful domestic sounds no more intrusive than the refrigerator hum of modern households. The wood burning stove roars out its warmth, popping when the flames hit pockets of pitch. Wall timbers snap, expanding and contracting from the heat indoors and the cold beyond. Water boils in the teapots, bouncing the scale around. Gaslights hiss, soft as a sigh, as faintly they glow in their fat glass globes. Our lazy dog Cujo snores regally, curled on the bed, tail over nose. On either side Stew and I sit reading among the crumbs of last night's snack, our backs propped by pillows, our legs making mountains and valleys of the quilts. These old journals I read, the blue-lined, wire-bound, coffee-stained editions, separate the years my memory tends to blend. Time moves so slowly here the past is easy to catch. I turn the pages until I come upon the entry I am looking for without quite knowing why: January 16, 1980. "Today I met Stew." What followed were two brave and crazy years full of the stuff we call adventure, two years that became the pivot point in my life.

When I met Stew I was thirty-eight, twice divorced (of course, it wasn't I that didn't try), and convalescing from yet a third failed relationship, this one with a significant other. I was living with my two children in Palm Springs, in a condo just down the street from the house I grew up in, a house my parents were still living in.

I had misspent my youth. As a child of a successful doctor, an internist, I had been given, as a matter of course, three sisters and a brother. I had been provided with orthodontia, ballet lessons, cello lessons, tennis lessons, and instruction on the care of fine china. I had been encouraged to go to the college of my choice to study whatever I wanted for as long as I wanted. At the several colleges and universities I did attend, I only picked up bits of education—biology, geology, geography, photography, creative writing — never graduating from any of them, never staying long enough, always moving from city to city, trying to shake my passionate restlessness.

Without a degree, without any real skills, I did not see vistas of opportunity opening before me. My career options were limited. So I went into banking. When Stew found me

I was the operations manager of a multi-branched bank. For eighteen years, like a machine, I had been counting other people's money, sorting it, stacking it, strapping it, the grime coming off on my fingers (I still have nightmares). What I had learned best in all those years was how to count money. The more money I counted, the less important it seemed. I was so sick of the sight of it, I grew casual, almost careless, about wealth.

I was living, or so it seemed at the time, the hellish life much of the human race accepts as its lot, with every hour assigned to work, meals, television, bed — alarm set for six. My weekends were marathons of cooking, washing, sweeping, dusting, grocery shopping — I was never surprised to see myself in the store at 11 p.m. — and dozens of tasks left undone and no time to be a mom, no time or energy to simply love the people I loved. I was so sick of it, the rushed mess of my life, the gush of humanity, the high cost of living, the ferocious summer heat, the smog, the snarled traffic, the tourists, the runaway crime. The more I thought about my life as it was, the more hopeless I found it to be. I felt my very soul was drying up cell by cell.

What kept me going were my annual vacations when I went beyond the interstate via packaged bird-watching tours. In Alaska I learned what wilderness was and a longing to live in the wilderness began coursing through my blood. I wanted to just throw myself out there and see if something wonderful might happen, out there in some wilderness with forests and deep grassy glades where you could rest in joy forever. I wanted to begin life again, to go country, go simple, go free. I wanted to grow my own food, to hike from my back door, to read all the books I always meant to read. As it was, books kept me going, books written by people who had traded their treadmill for life in the wilds (I picked up more than a few hints from Thoreau). With axes they built remote cabins. They lighted them with lanterns and swept them clean with a broom. The *Mother Earth News* taught them in loving detail whatever they couldn't work out for themselves, things like how to home school your kids, how to garden organically, how to build a greenhouse, a water ram, a fence.

But *Mother* didn't tell it all. This simple life was expensive. Ways of earning a living were limited to non-commuters, to writers, marijuana growers, and trust-fund beneficiaries. Nevertheless I began squirreling away my paychecks, hacking away at my budget, even though my goal was distant and far from clear.

Any real plan I remember having, or imagine I remember having, would have wound up in the fantasy bin had I not met Stew. It wasn't so much that I found him or he found me but that we were fated to meet. Into my troubled life at my very boring bank he appeared, presto!, one glorious day, taking the form of a bank customer, which isn't surprising considering he worked as a heavy equipment mechanic at the construction company catty-cornered to my bank. There he was standing at my desk, wanting me to balance his checkbook. He was such a handsome devil—silky blond hair, long narrow face, dimpled cheeks when he smiled, broad shoulders tapering down to slim hips, impressive muscles in his arms, not tall, but tall enough to fit his character, a strong man, a quiet man, a mountain man in the making. I looked into his eyes, very blue, slightly untamed, wide with wisdom (be still my heart), and I knew he was just the man to lead me through a wilderness full of great fanged beasts.

Good voices don't always belong to good looks, but Stew's did. Business concluded, he asked me the very question I had hoped he would. Dinner Saturday? I never could say no to destiny.

By candlelight we told each other our life histories right up to the moment of our meeting. "What's the most wonderful thing you've ever done?" The most awful, the most exciting, the most foolish–he told me and I told him. I wanted to ask him – too many things, things he could not have answered. We had a lot to learn about each other, far too much to know where to begin. He showed me snapshots from his wallet, all the while smiling with love, fatherly pride. Chad and Roy. Roy and Chad. Which was which. The boys looked identical, the blue in their eyes the same blue as Stew's, and the gold in their hair. There was a barely detectable upward tilt at the tip of all three noses. But then I saw how Roy had a saddle of freckles across his nose where in Chad there were none. Roy's eyes were cold sober, Chad's decidedly mischievous, full of the dickens.

Just months before we met, Stew had fled Phoenix, Arizona, leaving in his wake his career, most of his belongings, and his house in the suburbs, wherein still lived the reason for his fleeing, his ex-wife.

Stew and I did more dating, more dining out. We did a little dancing, a little drinking, and a lot of talking. But ours was scarcely a whirlwind romance. It was scarcely a romance at all. We discovered we weren't each other's types. Our backgrounds, our interests, and our tastes were poles apart. Our spoken language was barely the same. Plus which there was no animal magnetism between us. The chemistry wasn't right. When we kissed bells didn't ring, the earth didn't move, magical currents didn't pass between us. But we liked each other well enough. So we began dismantling our separate desperate lives. Whatever we were going to do we knew we were going to do it together. Beyond that we knew nothing.

I wanted to go to the wilderness, somewhere entirely undeveloped, unknown. Alaska was at the top of my list. But I don't remember if I was the one to suggest Alaska or Stew was. I don't remember discussing it at all. One week we just started getting Stew's pickup in shape for a long journey, we didn't know exactly where, we'd find out when we got there. Then I held a moving sale in the lunch room of the bank, sold my television, stereo, popcorn popper, hair dryer, dresses, shoe trees, everything I thought I would no longer need. My fellow workers looked hard into my face for traces of lunacy. My parents looked on in silent disapproval as I moved out of the condo I had been renting from them and into Stew's apartment. I sold my car. I quit my job and Stew quit his. Believe me, we left no bridge unburned. Sometimes I would come awake at night and wonder what I had in mind. Who did I think I was going off like this? I should stay here, make the best of things as they are. I was a mother for god's sake. Risking my own future was one thing. Risking my kids' future was something else. And just where did I think I was going anyway? What did I think I was going to do there — wherever — with the rest of my life? This was beyond comprehension. This was insane! The impossibility of it all overwhelmed me with excitement.

From the books I had read I knew exactly what to take on the trip. Packed beneath the camper shell of Stew's pickup were all the makings for a grand adventure: tents, sleeping bags, fishing poles, a moose gun, a grouse gun, a haphazard assortment of cast iron pots and pans, a kerosene lantern, an ax, a broom. Hitched to the pickup was a utility trailer with a hinged lid, a big plywood box on wheels, packed with Stew's tools and the boys' toys. Adjusting this and pushing that Stew managed to pack in the personal items I couldn't bear to part with. We were loaded and ready to go.

On a hot June day, shortly after breakfast, we said our good-byes, broke loose, set off for our version of *Walden Pond*. For the usual emotional reasons we said our good-byes quickly, everything else needing to be said having been said the weeks before, all that talk coming to nothing.

My ten-year-old son, so city-bound he didn't want to come, would live in Los Angeles with his dad. My daughter, just graduated from high school, led her own life, had her own plans, none of which included giving up shopping malls. Or did I just suppose this? Was it that in my furious rush to leave I forgot to even ask her to come? I was ditching my daughter and son is how my parents saw it. I was running off to the moon with a man I barely knew, seven years my junior and with two kids of his own, two toddlers I had not even met. I was disappointing my father. I was making my happy mother unhappy. Both of them were as confused about my leaving as I was, although they should have understood. If they hadn't struck out for it when they had been young, I would have been born in Kansas or Nebraska instead of California. What I mean is, I come from a long line of people who have moved around, all of us born travelers, meant to go places. Still, I wished I could have gone through this all by myself, without hurting anyone else.

Even so, my parents didn't expect me to be gone for very long. They gave me six months, a year at the most, to come back to reality, if you can call Palm Springs reality. After living in Riverside for a year, in San Francisco for two years, and in Los Angeles for six years, I had come back. It was just a matter of time before I would come home again and put my life back in order (putting my life back in order would certainly take some doing this time, having burned my bridges).

In my deepest truest heart I believed in what I was doing, and sometimes believing in something means you just believe in it. And yet I was none too confident as I drove off with this man I barely knew into a future that was a great unknown, saying goodbye to my past, calling goodbye to my son, my daughter, my mother, my father, waving goodbye, goodbye, goodbye, until my family, these loved ones I might never see again, fell far behind. Hundreds of miles later I realized the enormity of what I had done. I thought I would feel guilt, doubt, remorse, despair. I didn't. I thought I would be in shock. I wasn't, I had so much faith. If I could just pull this off, if I could just pull this off.

We didn't head for Alaska right away. Alaska would come later. As good luck would have it Stew's mom was baby-sitting Roy and Chad. So Bird City, Kansas, was where we went and picked up the boys, where we took the law into our hands and put ourselves hopelessly in the wrong.

Days later, with the boys seated between us, cassette popped into the player, windows rolled down to feel the wind, Stew and I drove off on our delicious adventure, heading for Alaska, that empty hinterland where even fools fear to tread. With wide-opened eyes we passed through Colorado, Montana, British Columbia, Yukon Territory, Northwest Territory, hundreds and hundreds of miles of unfamiliar landscape, a lot of emptiness in this crowded century. We were on no schedule. There was no place we had to be. We could camp for a few nights when we were tired of driving, for a few weeks when we had a lake all to ourselves. So by the time we reached Alaska months later I had grown to know Stew the man, Stew the father. But I hadn't gone so far as to love him yet. That would come later.

An August snowstorm, a serious snowstorm, caught us camping like gypsies in an abandoned public campground in Tok, Alaska. In another month we were living like pioneers in that same campground, in a tiny log cabin we had thrown together just to get us through the winter. But winter didn't go as planned. On Halloween, at the post office in Tok, we opened a telegram. The local cops wanted to see Stew, immediately. This sounded serious. At first we thought it might be because we were shooting grouse out of season, without a license. Then we thought it might be because we had built this cabin on BLM land. Then we thought about Stew's ex. Could it be that she . . . Nah! With us outlaws it could be any number of things.

As it turned out Stew was questioned about all of the above, but he was jailed for custodial interference. Ordinarily this would have been a misdemeanor, but having been committed across state lines, it was a felony. We had come to our reckoning. Everything we had worked for, so recklessly gambled for, blew up in our faces.

How Stew's ex managed to find us from her living room in Phoenix, Arizona, is unimportant and too tangled to unravel here. In a matter of days, under court order, we found ourselves tracing our route back through hundreds of miles of landscape that would have been familiar had it not been for all the snow. While I wintered in Palm Springs in the house of my parents, my childhood home, Stew attended hearings in Phoenix courtrooms. It was here that our luck ricocheted from abominable to sublime. With something as simple as a signature Stew's ex dropped the charges and gave custody of the boys to him.

All winter and spring, for a thousand empty days and a thousand lonely nights, Stew and I were separated from each other by hundreds of miles. He was busy working at a mine. I was busy working for my mother. I had no car. So only letters went back and forth between us. But through letters we discovered we had come to feel like a family, the four of us, or at least to feel family feelings for each other. And it was as a family we made our next plans.

Wilderness was now something Stew and I could no longer live without. So that June, with the pickup packed, the boys and their malamute pup seated between us, we

left for Alaska again, snuck away in the night, no witnesses, no good-byes.

We had jobs for the summer in the Brooks Range. Stew
had arranged it beforehand. He would be a driller at a gold
camp on Crooked Creek. I would be the camp cook.

Our home for the summer was a large canvas tent.
Here we spent the nights, or the non-working hours that
pass for night in this land of the midnight sun. Stew's long
days afield fixing, always fixing, the old exploratory drill
ended with dinner at eight. My long days in the cook shack
slaving over an old wood-burning range ended some time
after everyone in camp had been well-fed, or not so well-
fed to hear the complaints about my burned biscuits,
bloody-rare roasts, and failed lemon soufflés. It wasn't the
oven's fault, it was my fault, all of it. I am not blind to my
shortcomings. I have never been what you would call a
good cook. I have never been devoted to cooking even
under the best of circumstances. Nevertheless I was
putting up a brave effort here and it didn't seem to count.
Tolerating lousy cooks wasn't a strong point in this mining
camp. Crummy meals didn't so much stop these miners
from eating as make them mad. While I was never able to
nail down any actual death threats, the stories went
around, some of which scare me even in retrospect. I was
learning not so much how to cook but how much I hated
cooking.

So when the first week of October came around and
the water froze in the creeks, in the drill, in the sluice box
and no more work could be done, being laid off came as a
relief to me. Unfortunately during the summer Stew and I
had been so busy, so far from unemployment offices and
want ads and a telephone, we couldn't prepare for the coming winter. Once again we found ourselves unemployed,
homeless, without an address. Once again we left Alaska,
this time never to return.

We had a wad of wages though. So we bought something the four of us could live in temporarily, a large secondhand Airstream travel trailer with a kitchenette, a bathroom, a double bed, and twin bunks. Then we frittered away the rest of our pay wandering through Canada and the American Northwest, job hunting more or less, and looking for somewhere to settle, a place where the living was cheap and the scenery priceless. A home. For you see, now Stew was calling me Ma and I was calling him Pa. (We've been Ma and Pa ever since. To this day I have never understood what happened to our Christian names.)

In January we found that place although we didn't recognize it at first because of the blizzard. Following rumors of a hiring frenzy at a newly-opened molybdenum mine we blew into central Idaho on the tailwind of this blizzard, with hope and not much else. With less than three hundred dollars in our pockets, like it or not, this was where our grand adventure would come to its final end.

2
Challis, Idaho

I observed that the vitals of the village were the grocery, the bar-room, the post-office, and the bank; and, as a necessary part of the machinery, they kept a bell, a big gun, and a fire-engine, at convenient places; and the houses were so arranged as to make the most of mankind, in lanes and fronting one another, so that every traveller had to run the gantlet, and every man, woman, and child might get a lick at him.
    –Henry David Thoreau

Custer County, Idaho
Named for George Armstrong Custer.
Region first settled by miners.
Over 93 percent federally owned.
Population density .8 persons per square mile.
Households number approximately 2,400.
Businesses number approximately ninety.

There are no stoplights in Custer County, an area the size of Connecticut. There are no radio stations or fast-food franchises or chain stores. The children living in Clayton attend a one-room school. The children living in Stanley, having no school of their own, ride a bus to Challis, two hours and fifteen minutes away. According to the town elderlies and local boosters this remoteness, this isolation, is why progress has passed on by.

That ranching drives the machinery of Custer County is maddeningly obvious to travelers who have to thread their way through cattle drives on Scenic Byway 93. Riverfront ranches and vistas of cows stretch wide on both sides of the pavement, clear to the sagebrushed aprons of the mountains. Cow dogs appear from nowhere, galloping alongside your wheels, taking a run at your wheels, pulling up just short of having their paws pasted to the pavement. As you near Challis you can't help hearing the roar of rodeo crowds as real, spur-heeled buckaroos thunder out the chutes and rassle steers to the ground.

Challis, Idaho, 83226.
Seat of Custer County.
Founded by Alvah P. Challis, cattleman, miner, entrepreneur.
Once served as the main freight terminal for all mining districts in the southern half of Salmon River Country.

In the tiny town of Challis and in the huge county around it there is only one jail. Dubbed the "Custer Hilton," it is located behind the courthouse on Main Street. Built in 1913, this incredibly small humble stone building contains only four cells, that's four single-bed cells. The inmates with kitchen privileges cook their own meals using vegetables the dispatcher brings from her garden and meat from elk and deer roadkilled (fresh, not putrid) or confiscated from local poachers.

Adjoining the jail, hiding its beautiful old stonework, is a modular building with aluminum siding and the kind of plastic paneling that is supposed to look like wood. This is the office of the Custer County Sheriff. In the lobby there's a front desk where you go to report automobile accidents, be they car/car collisions or car/cow collisions or

Challis, Idaho

car/deer collisions. Here you file complaints when you discover your mailbox bashed in, your automobile tires slashed, and your lawn littered with party garbage. Down the hall from the lobby, in several small offices, the sheriff and his deputies look into the hows, whys, and wherefores of what little real crime takes place in Challis. The *Challis Messenger* reports these crimes and other nonsense as well.

Item: A Challis Creek resident called to report that "someone had cut his horse's mane and tail and spray painted one side of the horse green and the other side of the horse red." Deputy Twitchell is investigating.

Item: A Challis woman called to say two ceramic bunnies had been stolen from her lawn. Officer Nelson was able to recover the bunnies.

Item: Twitchell was called to track down three young males and one female on Trail Creek Road who were seen taking street signs.

Item: A woman called complaining her son was trying to hit her daughter's toe with a knife.

It's these kids nowadays, these teenagers for whom mischief is the only game in town. They haven't managed to make for themselves a full life out of living in small town society, a society they find about as interesting as oatmeal mush. To hear them whine, if they could choose the life they would most like to live, they would choose any life but the one they are living. So it isn't surprising that after graduating from high school (or not graduating as the case may be), they rush to get out of this hellhole town and into the fast life of the cities. The ranks of young people are thinning, even of those tied by tradition to family ranches. Nevertheless, the traditional western industries are thriving here, as they are thriving in the rest of the West, and not just ranching, but mining as well, even as the newly-found tourist industry is beginning to form.

Challis owes its beginning to mining and not much else. Mining is still very much alive thanks in part to the construction crews who built the Thompson Creek Molybdenum Mine forty miles from Challis. In 1981, these crews came and created a social upheaval not seen since the gold rush days of the century before.

"Too many people, too much change, too much money, too much frustration, too many burdens on people and institutions not able to respond quickly enough to the demands." The *Challis Messenger* editorialized the chaos. The network news reported it to the nation, filmed it, the trailers jammed together at all the mobile home parks, ninety trailers at Saturday Mountain Resort, a park designed for eight. Only six portable privies had been

brought in to serve the overflow. During a hepatitis out-
break, health inspectors noted mounds of yellow snow and
declared that six toilets weren't nearly enough.

On January 5th, 1982, we arrived in Challis, blissfully
ignorant of this chaos, our employment hopes hitched to
the Thompson Creek Mine. Through the blizzard Stew
drove with squinty-eye concentration. Our trailer, our
home in tow, was wrecked from traveling across Canada's
pothole-pitted back roads. The frame was fractured under
the bathroom door and all hell could break loose any
minute. The bathroom window, having been smashed by
flying rocks, was plugged with plywood. It let in the awful
cold. The stove, having somehow separated itself from the
wall, kept walking across the kitchenette, across the living
room, stopping just short of busting out the door.

In a word we were trailer-busted as we slid along
Scenic Byway 93, passing log cabins boarded up, long emptied of homesteaders, their apple orchards dying, their corrals fallen down, passing junkyards of rusted mine
machinery and rusted farm machinery, passing gas stations and motels, a little bush-hopper airport, the first-aid
station, the small country churches, the big Mormon
church, the bowling alley, the city park, and the big official
sign proclaiming Challis "Gateway to the Wilderness."
Looking for a real estate office we turned up deserted
Main Street. It looked much too wide with no traffic to fill
it.

Makeshift real estate offices were everywhere and all
open for business in spite of the storm. Stew parked the
truck in the front yard of an old log home where Heads Up
Hair Salon shared a living room with Must See Realty. We
crossed the front porch, passing flower pots, their flowers
frozen, stone dead. We whooshed through the door, clomp-
clomping snow across the carpet. Behind a desk the realtor sprang to life, rubbing his hands, grinning his wide

searchlight grin, stepping forward to pump Stew's hand, crushing Stew's hand, so happy to see us. He seated us at his desk, served us coffee and doughnuts, saw to our every comfort. All the while he appraised us with the subtlety of a starving shark.

Grubby as we were, well-trampled by our adventure, creased and greasy-faced, wrinkled and woozy from weeks on the road, I suppose we looked no worse than the rest of the riffraff, the miners with jobs and paychecks. In any case the realtor went into his routine beginning with how much we were going to like living here, the clean fresh air, the swimming holes for the kids, the streams full of fish, the forests full of elk, running on and on until he ran out of ecstasies. "Whatever you want we got it. You're real lucky you came in today. Got just one lot left in Rancho Del Rio. Got some river frontage left in Whispering Snakes Estates. This is priced to sell real quick. Got a real cute cabin on Challis Crick, that's the way he said it, "crick," he showed us pictures. It's got a two-car garage, a wrap-around redwood deck, electric baseboard heat, satellite dish, blah, blah, blah."

This monologue would have gone on indefinitely but for a blare from our truck, Chad horsing around. Swiveling his chair away from us, the realtor stared out the window, his pitch simply petering out. There was our wrecked trailer, our truck caked with mud, staring out its cracked headlights. Out the cracked windshield stared the pup, begging someone to free him from the yards of toilet paper Chad had wrapped him in. Oh, Chad, Chad, Chad. Two straws stuck up his nose, his mouth a clown's mouth of red lipstick, his cheeks puffed with air, like a hippopotamus. With his fists he punched the air out of his cheeks, refilled them, and crossed his eyes at us when he caught us watching. I saw how the realtor was not even a little bit amused. The wretched truth of our predicament had come to him at last. With a gawd-help-me sigh he swiveled back to business. "Tell you what. I'll make you a deal on a fix-it-upper. Needs a little work is all, on the roof and the plumbing." What he had in mind was most likely something that should have been condemned rather than listed.

With my knee I nudged Stew, the spokesman for our motley crew. "Uh, got any apartments for rent?"

The realtor sat silent for a moment, stunned. Cigarette smoke spiraled from his ashtray, clung to the ceiling, and seemed to ooze from every opening of his head. His searchlight grin had long since gone dim. Now his eyebrows twisted and writhed. "Gawd, it's been months, years, since we've had anything for rent in this town." With that he became deeply involved in filling his stapler. This sorry business had come to an end.

Welcome to Challis, you bet! There were other real estate offices we could have checked, but the thought of more cigarette smoke, more discouragement, kept us from doing so. Instead we drove up and down the neighborhoods where houses were arranged fronting one another so that every traveler had to run the gantlet. Nothing moved in the streets, life having withdrawn into the houses sealed tight against the storm. Not much was going on indoors either. In fact, it appeared our arrival was the only thing going on. Kitchen curtains parted in curiosity as slowly we pass, looking for a FOR RENT sign but finding nothing. We went to the *Messenger* and scanned the classifieds for rentals. Nothing there either. Looking for rumors of rentals we went to Bux's Bar, sat on stools in the barroom gloom, drinking beers elbow-to-elbow with other serious drinkers. While seventeen dusty dead animal heads looked down from the wall, looked down in disapproval, we dipped our fingers into jars of pickled eggs, turkey gizzards, and Hot Mama Sausages, wanting to keep up our strength for our eventual return to the cruel winter streets. Every half hour or so we ran bags of potato chips out to the boys who had been ordered to take their naps in the truck. Somehow the afternoon just slipped away and with it, our troubles.

Out the door we floated and into early evening. Luck had been kind to us, sort of. After listening to our beery laments the bartender had steered us toward a parking lot recently converted into a trailer park, located at the intersection of Highway 93 and Main. The trailer sites were way in back, behind the old Suds 'n Spin. Here we found a vacant site, only one, vacated just hours before we arrived. The manager warned us the water lines had broken from the cold and couldn't be fixed until the ground thawed in spring. Nonetheless he charged us his going rate, a rate inflated by the mining boom, a rate we could ill afford. Stew and I chewed on this for a few seconds, let our minds digest it. We were out of money, out of highway, out of luck. There would be no more little escapades into the wilderness. We took the site, reassuring ourselves it was only temporary, just a matter of a few days, a week at the most.

As it turned out the dreary backside of that launderette was our view for nine weeks, five days, and three hours (I recorded every miserable day in my journal). The water lines were indeed broken, so every morning we filled our ice chest with water from the launderette and dipped out what we needed for cooking, coffee, dish washing, flushing the toilet. Every few days a roll of quarters got us showers.

Even so, these inconveniences were minor compared to the huge inconvenience caused when the trailer's toilet flusher froze one sub-zero night. In a fit of frustration, Stew, ever willing to attack a 4-penny finish nail with a sledgehammer, hammered too hard, broke the sumbitch contraption, and declared it unrepairable. To my horror, Stew sawed a hole in the bathroom floor, hooked the hole to the sewer hose, and all February we went in a big metal funnel.

Were there any good times at all? I don't think so. Mostly we just tried to survive. An irritable journal entry I scribbled one evening about sums it up. "It's minus thirty-six degrees outside. Inside we all sit in our coats, huddled around the portable heater, the oven on broil, all burners ablaze. And still we are c-c-cold."

That Stew would be hired by the mine was inevitable. He was very good at what he did. It was just a matter of waiting until someone quit or was fired. And in late February he was hired, told to report for work in mid-March. Until then, to keep warm, to pass time, to stay sane, we walked the streets and got to know this town we found. We walked with Roy on his daily pilgrimage to first grade. Chad, crushed at being too young for kindergarten, just a few weeks on the wrong side of the deadline, walked with us among the clumps of little kids bound for school, the girls giggling and whispering, the boys cat-calling and bashing each other with lunchboxes. Chad walked with the pup on a leash, the pup being just the right prop he needed to gain entrance into kid society. Well Chad didn't exactly walk. Chad never walked. He lagged far behind or sprinted way ahead, twirled, skipped, danced, dragging the balky pup along, skidding her along on her bottom.

Leaving happy school, returning to dreary trailer park, Chad was often quiet, no not quiet, Chad was never that, but sort of sulky, withdrawn, glum. Stew and I were just as reluctant to return. So we took the long way back, the roundabout route, up North Street, down Pleasant Street, up Valley, down Butte. We passed abandoned log cabins and more log cabins that weren't abandoned but should have been, all hunkering down below peaks packed with snow and bluffs raw and rocky, rising in ranks of orange, green, and brown. Smoke rose curling from the chimneys of homes built in the 1880s and lovingly restored in soft shades of yellows and blues. Pink plastic flamingos stretched tall-legged above one snowy lawn that ran clear to the shelf ice on Garden Creek. The frozen stubble of last summer's cornrows ran to groves of trees, their branches leafless and stiff as quills, their trunks wrapped in tape against the gnawing hunger of rodents. These trees would bear the blossoms of apples and plums should spring ever come again. A dear old lady told us this. She had come out from behind her parted curtains. She wanted to meet us, those new people from California.

Down the alleys we went, where the smells of break-fast cooking lingered and small dogs came barking out back doors and stuck their noses through the slats of white frozen fences, eager to meet the new pup in town. Down Main Street we went. Traffic was so light you could cross safely without looking either way. The sidewalks were deserted except for a few grandfathers out walking their ratty old dogs, lonely old men who half-nodded to us as we half-nodded to them. Main Street was silent except for the thin music of wind chimes and the chatter of winter birds gleaning seeds from rows of giant sunflowers, sunflowers that served as fences for more lovely old homes, these sharing sidewalk space with the vitals of the village, the grocery, the barroom, the post office, the bank, and the not-so-vitals of the village, the beauty shops, the boutiques, the video rentals, and the real estate offices we would watch come and go.

Back to the trailer for lunch, then back to Main Street, now as busy as it had been deserted earlier. We needed to check things out. The realtor might have a new listing, the *Messenger* a new ad, the post office a letter from home. Also we needed to get out of that lousy trailer and back into the bustling heart of town.

The crusin' crowd from the high school was out for

lunch, revving up the engines of their rifle-racked 4x4s, squealing their tires, doing doughnuts down Main. Occasionally, the Challis Volunteer Fire Department went squealing around the corners in their trucks, bright red relics from the not so distant past. Whether there was a real fire or just a fire drill, whether it was noon or not noon, the noon siren would sound off with a series of shrieks that melted the wax in your ears and set to howling every backyard dog.

People were everywhere, merchants, clerks, ranchers, miners, housewives shopping, paying their bills, getting their mail, getting their hair cut, lunching at Bux's, lunching at Antonio's, lunching at the Copper Kettle Cafe where the clatter of plates came out the door with aromas of down-home country cooking. People were doing their banking, visiting the dentist, visiting each other, actually sitting on a bench out front of the Custer Saloon. Everyone seemed to know everyone else, or thought they did anyway. And well they might have. Some of them were related, their families having lived here for decades, if not generations. Some of them were neighbors, their gardens connected by the risky foot bridges of Garden Creek. Some of them were friends, their interests connected by clubs of all sorts, clubs for art lovers and bridge players and bowlers and history nuts and clubs only for the lonely.

Just to be doing something until it was time for Roy to be set free, we walked down one side of Main Street and up the other, the passerbys smiling to our smiles. Sometimes we browsed through the dozen or so false-fronted stores, most of them well over a hundred years old and still standing, still doing business, not as usual but in modern ways, selling satellite dishes, hot tubs, and trampolines. Twin Peaks Sports sold things that could be used for miles around, on the rivers, at the lakes, in the forests. Jan's Gifts sold useless things, whoopee cushions, snapsnots, canned jack rabbit milk (unsweetened). Stew and I would come to own these gifts when Chad learned to save his Saturday dollars. Perfect for Mother's Day. Won't Mom be surprised. I think I could have lived a fulfilled life without a slab of rubber vomit.

Spring came at the end of March, along with Stew's first paycheck, along with a single-wide trailer house for rent, all of which were sorely needed. In a matter of a day we were moved into this trailer, this aluminum-sided eyesore parked permanently among the noxious weeds of a vacant lot. This eyesore of a lot was located in a neighborhood of carefully mowed lawns and tidy flower beds, a neighborhood that looked mighty neighborly. Much to Chad's delight the trailer was right across the street from Challis Elementary. Much to our distress, where we thought we had rented living space, in truth, we had rented a wreck of mice nests and broken waterpipes and leaky roofing and untrustworthy furniture with frayed threads and dark stains, leftovers from someone else's life. The carpet, an ancient shag, in a puce shade, was worn bald around the heating stove where people had stood to warm themselves. The couch, a miserable piece of cracked black plastic patched with electric tape, puffed stuffing whenever we sat down.

As shabby as it was, as in bad need of repair, compared to the Airstream, it looked like a castle, these tiny, unloved rooms. For the next two years we rented it in disrepair, then bought it, still in disrepair, for twice what it was worth. After another year we sold it in disrepair for the same price. We also sold the Airstream, also in disrepair, for twice what it was worth. It was that kind of real estate market back then, that kind of boom.

During those three years in Challis, Stew's world was defined by day shifts, night shifts, double-shifts, and hour-long rides to the mine and hour-long rides from the mine, first aboard the big blue bus, then later on, when he was promoted, aboard the supervisors' van. Also during this time, Stew and I stopped living in sin. We got married at the courthouse, a five-minute ceremony, the judge's secretary and a clerk our only witnesses. No rings. No reception. No honeymoon — Stew had to get back to work. Nevertheless, we made my mother happy and Stew's mother happy. We were no longer just Jo and Stew. We were the Churchwells.

With the benefit of hindsight I see how Stew's work, his shifts, his goings and comings, defined my world too, as did Loony Tunes, fluoride treatments, scout meetings. I spent every season in a world not of my choosing, in a world not of nature's making, but on the sidelines cheering Roy through baseball marathons or in the kitchen whipping up dozens of pink Valentine cakes for Chad's kindergarten class or at Jan's Gifts buying Chad a monster mask or in the jungle-humid gym, scowling at Chad in his elf costume shooting death rays out his fingers during the singing of *Silent Night*.

"Oh, Chad, Chad, Chad, what have you done now? What now?" I chanted this every time I was summoned to school. I got summoned to school a lot. I got to know the principal's office real well. Chad was always failing half his subjects, always fooling around, messing around with the rules of proper behavior. He had too much animal energy is what his teachers thought. He was inconsiderate, disruptive, up to no good, always talking in class, turning his class work into gliders, sailing them at the other kids, spitballing the other kids, playing jokes on his teachers, rubber spiders, plastic eyeballs. More than once the principal had paddled him to give his message force. Of course Chad just kept doing those things, especially because he wasn't supposed to, he had been punished, he had been warned. The principal just shook his head. Chad was incurable.

On the playground he dynamited his way into school society, turning games into fist fights. I would watch him playing catch with himself or swinging on the swings, trying to get attention, swinging himself sick, swinging higher and higher until I feared he would swing full circle. I watched him at the baseball diamond. I saw how the boys, in choosing up sides, always left Chad the last to be chosen or not chosen at all, learning defeat, learning early his role in life.

It wasn't that Chad was bad the principal told me again and again. Chad was just maladjusted, disoriented, unmotivated, in need of guidance. He was lacking in continued success toward integration of his personality as a social unit (or something like that, I forgot his exact words).

As Chad was never part of school society Stew and I were never part of Challis society, even as we enthusiastically attended school functions, PTA meetings, parties and picnics hosted by the Thompson Creek Mine. When we went to the Custer Saloon to celebrate this or that, we went alone. In our Wild West hats and pointy-toed boots we looked like everyone else out there on the dance floor. But as we clogged with the other clogging couples we never cut much of a figure. We never learned to move our feet to the fiddle bands. We always danced best alone, in the dark.

There were never any overtures of friendship from our neighbors, as if we Churchwells were just passing through and not here to stay (the only people who ever used our front door were the Jehovah's Witnesses). I was never invited to Tupperware parties or fudge bake-offs or even to just share the latest kitchen gossip. I was not touchy about this. There was no great sorrow in my soul. Really, I didn't mind at all that the neighbors were unknown to me except as closed doors I passed on my morning birdwalks. I am telling this not in a rush of self-pity but to explain why, when tragedy struck Custer County on the morning of October 28, 1983, Stew and I were the last to know. No one rushed over. Our telephone never rang.

Being a native of Southern California I have a most intimate relationship with the infamous San Andreas family of faults. I have rocked through more than my fair share of major earthquakes. So that morning, as Stew lay sleeping between shifts, first on the bed, then quite suddenly, off the bed, as the boys and I were trying to keep our cereal bowls from crashing to the floor, I knew this earthquake was the most major earthquake I had ever experienced. It wasn't so much the noise indoors, which was scary enough considering the trailer's matchbox construction, but the noise outdoors, the noon siren, the fire truck sirens, the ambulance sirens, the whomp-whomp-whomp of the helicopters overhead. There was so much smoke. The whole town was in flames is what we thought.

As we learned later, through the pages of the *Messenger*, their special award-winning earthquake edition, this was not smoke at all but dust thick as smoke. In a haze of disbelief we read how the bluffs around Challis had shaken, sending boulders the size of pickups bouncing down, crashing down on buildings and parked cars and four of Bill Yacomella's pigs. Lawana Knox, out hunting elk near the Mount Borah epicenter, found herself hanging horrified to a sagebrush as power poles bent and snapped apart like toothpicks, as the ground swelled beneath her, cracked open in front of her "like someone had taken scissors to a piece of paper and just cut it."

Through the *Messenger* we learned what had caused all the commotion on Main Street just after the earthquake. Standing next door to Jan's was what folks called the "Old Company Store." It had been built in the century before from rocks quarried near the bluffs overlooking the store. These rocks had been bonded with some kind of insubstantial stuff made in the old lime kiln at the edge of town. On the morning of the Borah Peak Quake, the store was being used only as a storage facility. It was structurally unsound, in bad need of condemning, and all but inviting the tragedy it caused when it collapsed on the sidewalk in a pile of rubble.

Over a dozen people ran to the scene, began heaving rubble out of the way. One witness was amazed at the speed with which everyone worked and the size of the rocks they moved by hand. "We were all hoping against hope that they weren't there—that it was all a terrible mistake." In fact, both kids, seven-year-old Tara Leaton and six-year-old Travis Franck, had been killed instantly.

It wasn't long before the reporters and camera crews swooped down on the town, some from as far away as New York. What followed can best be described as a media feeding frenzy in which the Borah Peak Quake was brought dramatically to the nation's attention. You would search far and wide to find more impressive earthquake statistics. Measuring 7.3 on the Richter Scale, this was the largest quake to rock the continental United States in twenty-four years. It left a 20-mile-long escarpment at the base of Mount Borah. Here the valley floor dropped 7.5 feet and Mount Borah (at 12,662 feet, the highest point in Idaho) rose a foot.

Days later, as the reporters and crews were looking for their way home, talk throughout the shell-shocked neighborhoods still focused on the earthquake. Where were you when it happened? What were you doing? Did you have much damage to your house? At some time or other just about everyone in town toured the epicenter, including, should you be wondering, Stew and me. With our neighbors we gaped at the gap and posed our kids along the rim of it, trying to give some measure to it, some sense of awesomeness our cameras were incapable of capturing.

Later still the Challis National Forest published an even more impressive statistic: the Borah Peak Quake had triggered the largest upsurging of ground water ever recorded following an earthquake in the United States. During the quake, sand had been hurled into the air, then sand and water, then water and mud, until a string of forty ponds stretched across the Lost River Valley. The hydrological system was so topsy-turvy the Clayton Silver Mine flooded and Ingram's Warm Springs Creek stopped flowing altogether, stranding hundreds of fish on the dry creek bed. After dozens of aftershocks, the water in the creek returned, came gushing back at ten times its former flow. So Will Ingram, having abandoned his fish-farming venture, now supplies Utah Power with hydroelectricity.

After hundreds of aftershocks, one as recently as a month ago, I now have a most intimate relationship with the infamous Lost River family of faults.

Sustained violence, much of it volcanic in nature, created the knockout scenery in this country. Around forty-five million years ago explosions hundreds of times more powerful than the 1980 Mount Saint Helens eruption blasted ash and debris three hundred cubic miles around Van Horn Peak, the very same Van Horn Peak that serves as the centerpiece for our vista on Sawmill Creek. But it wasn't this vista, this joyously undisciplined landscape, that lured us here when our desire to live in the wilderness returned, digging itself in even deeper. It wasn't the privacy or the elbow room or all that wild food for the taking. You see, we chose Sawmill Creek by instinct, by inkling, much like our dog Cujo chose his best spot on the porch. It just felt right.

Sometime during our years in Challis Stew and I

began forming a plan, a jim dandy plan, the very best. We figured out how we could buy some property, build a house on it, and live there without wages, partly in self-sufficiency, partly in poverty, our sole income being the interest earned on our savings account. We made up our minds to be poor forever, to become experts at making do. When this plan progressed beyond the dream stage we began stockpiling Stew's paychecks, paychecks made chunky with overtime. By scrimping and scraping and just generally doing without we substantially increased our already substantial savings account. There would be no more borrowing, buying on time. Our follies of spending were over. We had the telephone disconnected, the cable service cut off. Instead of driving we walked. We stopped eating out and buying clothes new. "Sorry," I said to the Girl Scouts. "No cookies for us this year."

At Dreamchaser Realty we plunked down a princely sum, eighteen thousand dollars, cold hard cash. We took title to the upper end of an old homestead on Sawmill Creek, an island of privately-owned land surrounded by hundreds of square miles of public land administered by the Challis National Forest. We bought only five acres but we owned Sawmill Canyon, all of it, the ground, underneath the ground, the creek, the fish in the creek, the forests, the elk in the forests, the sun and moon and stars. Everything. There was no one around to say otherwise. There were no neighbors within shouting distance.

Then we started buying things we would need for our new life (we also bought things we wouldn't need). At farm auctions and estate auctions, when auctioneer Junior Baker raced through tables of old valuable things, Stew outbid everyone, which is how we came to own hammers and saws, rakes and hoes, buckets and washtubs, a flatiron and a pitcher pump. How we came to own things of questionable value, things that were chipped and twisted and missing their vital parts, goes something like this: "Whadya say, who'll give me ten dollars, ten dollars, ten dollars, all right then, six-six-six. Going, going, GONE! to Mr. Churchwell for fifty cents."

Our break with society came earlier than planned. One week the mine slashed production quotas, along with Stew's salary, just like that. So Stew upped and quit, just like that. We had been longing to be on the loose. We were ready to move to Sawmill Creek, ready to home school the boys, ready to build our log cabin, or ready enough anyway.

These days Challis no longer defines our world, our day-to-day living. But Challis still figures largely in our life. Once a month, during the snow free seasons, we drive the distance, twenty-five bone-bruising miles, for supplies and library books, for community functions and town meetings. In the aisles of the market, in the lobby of the bank, in line at the post office, we sharpen our social skills with people who believe, and rightly so, that we Churchwells have no one to talk to except the wild birds and beasts. In the town's eyes, as the years go by, we have become the Old Hippies of Sawmill Creek, an image, by the way, we do not dislike.

Times change. Towns change. But not Challis. Or I should say Challis hasn't changed enough to notice. The strip of businesses along Scenic Byway 93 is no uglier, and motorists can still lift their eyes to the mountains. Cars and houses are still left unlocked without resulting in disaster. Throughout the neighborhoods, among cabbages growing in perfect rows and old yellow roses blooming untended despite eight years of drought, the new satellite dishes look strangely out of place, like something Martians might have left behind after an invasion. With house prices spiraling insanely upward then downward then upward as the economy bounces from boom to bust to

Moonset over Van Horn Peak

back, the real estate offices still look as though they are capable of disappearing as quickly as they came.

But to hear folks talk, portents of change are evident. Across picket fences, on street corners, at Bux's Bar, they're saying the Californians are coming, and after them, the condos, the Kmarts, the traffic, the smog, the crime. By carloads they're coming, searching for their own private Idaho, turning tradition-bound towns like Challis into something like what they left behind. Stew and I hear this talk but we ignore it, or rather, we choose to disbelieve it. If in fact the Californians are coming we can't see them from our porch.

3
The Cabin

*I learned this, at least, by my experiment; that
if one advances confidently in the direction of his
dreams, and endeavors to live the life which he has
imagined, he will meet with a success unexpected
in common hours . . . . If you have built castles in
the air, your work need not be lost; that is where
they should be. Now put the foundations under
them.*
–Henry David Thoreau

Building a house is one of those deals where a guy ought
to have a little experience. And he ought to have the
proper heavy equipment. And he ought to have a proper
crew. Stew had none of the above. He had no experience
whatsoever in masonry or framing or roofing or cabinet-
making. He had no backhoe for digging, no crane for raising the walls and the roof, no cement mixer, no welder, no
power tools. For a crew he had us, two little kids and a
fumble-fisted wife.

Had Stew been a king he wouldn't have wanted a castle, or what serves today as a castle in resorts like Sun
Valley. Certainly, the magnificent Salmon River
Mountains surrounding us would have subdued any pre-
tentiousness built into the place. So with no argument
from me and with hardly any discussion, Stew decided to
build something small, simple, and architecturally
insignificant. No round-arched windows, no gingerbread

eaves, no fancy peaked cornices, no fancy shutters that do not shut, no walk-in fireplace, in fact, no fireplace at all, fireplaces being hopelessly inefficient compared to airtight stoves. With a porch on the west end, with both a greenhouse and a sun deck on the south end, we would have luxury enough just being able to sit in the sunshine anytime of day, anytime of year.

Where, exactly, our home should be built is where we had much discussion and more than a few arguments. Stew, ever practical, wanted to build in the meadow beside Sawmill Creek, where the driveway ended, where water would be handy. Sure we might feel a bit squeezed in by the hillsides but the building site was already level and landscaped with wildflowers, shade trees, and a lawn.

Ah, but if we built into the south-facing hillside, about thirty feet up from the creek, what a view, what a long, long view. I said this as if a view justified everything — having to hire a bulldozer to cut out the site, to level the site, to extend the driveway to the site, and all that landscaping we'd have to do so the site wouldn't wash away. Besides which, we'd have to haul water to the site, or Stew would, hauling water being man's work. Well, if it didn't kill him, it would certainly make him stronger, more manly.

In discussions of this sort I have always been able to go Stew one better. I am not given to budging. In this case my own tenacity astounded even me. As if he were about to dive underwater Stew took a deep breath and gave in to my whim. Yes. Yes! A home on the hillside it would be.

While Stew had been working for Thompson Creek Mine, between shifts, instead of sleeping, he made dozens of drawings of how our dream house would look, top to bottom, inside and out. He had sheets full of figures and solved problems (oh, the mysterious calculations of a builder's life). There were foundation details, every cinderblock drawn to scale. There were side views of all the log courses and various views of the rafters and the roof. There were floor plans detailed down to where the stoves would go, where the groceries would be put while we took off our coats, how many inches would go between the toilet and bathtub, well, you get the picture.

For twenty-five thousand dollars we turned Stew's artwork into a home, a log rectangle twenty-five feet wide, thirty-five feet long, capped with a roof of galvanized steel. Interior walls of tongue-and-groove pine divide the northern half of the house into a bathroom and two bedrooms (Stew and I now use the bedrooms as offices, one for him, one for me, his 'n' hers). Above the northern half of the house, the loft, extending from gable end to gable end, overlooks the sunny southern half of the house, an open space, two stories high, that serves as our living room and eat-in kitchen. As you might expect, throughout the house, there are large picture windows for the views I wanted—my folly, exclusively — windows we curtain only against the cold. Like Thoreau we have no gazers to shut out, only the sun and moon, and we are more than willing they should look in.

The western windows frame the sunset and the sunset porch and the hills beyond, tier upon tier of hills, some near, some far, all of them rolling upward to Van Horn Peak and a file of lesser peaks, a view I can photograph from bed. The southern windows look down upon the sun deck and the greenhouse and the view beyond, the great sweeping view of Sawmill Creek and its aspen groves, shady in summer, splendid in fall. More hills and ridges and peaks fill the eastern windows and in spring, showy spans of blue lupine, yellow balsamroot, white wyethia and in winter, thick stands of firs, their boughs down-swooping, heavy with snow.

The one and only northern window, installed to let

light into the bathroom, stares out at the clothesline, the woodpile, the stacks of cinderblocks and slate leftover from building the house, and the small battered Bell travel trailer we lived in while building the house. Since the trailer is mouseproof, nowadays, we use it as a dumpster for the garbage we have to store in winter when we are snowbound. In summer we use it for guests, after giving it a good airing. And in fall we use it for camping whenever we get these ridiculous urges to go sight-seeing in Yellowstone Park.

This Bell trailer is half the size of the Airstream, its scarred and stained linoleum floor measuring just six steps long and four steps wide. With great effort the divan converts into a double bed designed for Munchkins. There's a three-burner stove and a watch-it-bake-and-burn oven. There's a gaslight barely bright enough for reading. There's one small table we have to cover with pots and pans when it rains–weatherproof this trailer ain't. Nevertheless we called it home for almost three years, that is to say, for three building seasons at Sawmill and two winters in the desert southwest.

While we were building the house, this trailer was conveniently parked in the meadow below the building site. Through small screened windows came the sweet summer breezes, the perfume of wild lilies, and the fluting song of the thrush nesting in the willows on Sawmill Creek. Every morning Chad took the ice chest to the creek and fill it with water deliciously untreated, swimming with whirligig beetles and water boatmen all vigorously alive. We closed our eyes to the small black leeches clinging to the sides of our Sierra cups. We toughened our guts to the unicellular animals, the microcooties, that assured us the water was unpolluted, unchlorinated, and quite safe to drink. I can see my dear mother cringing as she reads this. Having been a doctor's wife all her adult life and being still

very much afraid of germs, she would rather I not write
this kind of stuff. And here I go announcing it to the entire
English-speaking world.

Something else my mother would rather I not mention
is that the trailer had no toilet. So here we were just
moved to Sawmill Creek, all of us eager to begin building
the house, and Stew says wait, first we have to build an
outhouse. He wanted it built high on the hillside opposite
the building site, deep within the fir forest, and it was here
he drew a circle with his shovel and directed the boys to
dig. They dug. Grumble-grumble-grumble. Into the soft
earth they dug, around and around, deeper and deeper,
their hands getting blistered and sore. When the hole was
well dug, Stew jumped in, measured it, and climbed back
out. "Dig deeper, boys."

When the hole was eight feet deep, Stew spanned it
with an old splintered two-by-four. We could sit on this
board temporarily, just until he got around to building the
rest of the outhouse (the commode, the log walls, the tin
roof, and the chimney that would vent the fumes). Well,
with Stew there is nothing more permanent than something temporary. As it turned out this outhouse you could-
n't tell from a hole in the ground served us for what
seemed a terribly long time.

Before building the house we also had to build two
sheds, two slant-roof shacks. And we did that. We painted
both sheds barn red. The shed on the hill at the edge of the
yard stores the tools Stew uses to build things and repair
things and the tools I use to hoe, weed, and water the garden. The shed below the hill at the end of the driveway
holds our snowshoes, skis, mountain bikes, and most of our
food and supplies.

Before building the house we also had to build a rail
fence along the west side and north side of our property
where our five acres abut another fifty acres or so of pri-

vate pasture (the absentee landlord rents this out to Rancher Rick for his cows). Our property came with a nasty barbed wire fence already installed on the south side, separating our property from the Challis National Forest, whose wild pastures are rented out, every two summers out of three, to the Morgan Creek Permittees: Rancher Will, Rancher Verl, Rancher Jim — well, the names don't matter. A few years ago the Challis Ranger District built a five-acre rail enclosure along the east side of our property, where the creek comes in. They built it, at our nagging insistence, to protect our water supply from all these cows. In spite of this fencing, it was inevitable that Stew and I would learn to hate cows with a hatred bigger than all our other hatreds (I'm not about to go into that now, which isn't to say I won't go into it later).

After building the outhouse, the two sheds, and the fence we would have started building the house if the cows had not kicked over the pole holding up our mailbox. After an hour of searching we found the missing mailbox kicked halfway to Corral Creek, lying in a ditch, missing its cheerful red flag, and considerably flatter than before. Amazingly the letters inside were undamaged.

We bought a new mailbox. Stew threw away the flimsy pole it came with and used a post leftover from building the fence. He planted the bottom of the post in cement. With steel, he bracketed the new mailbox on top. It worked. With cows anyway. But as we were soon to discover, rural mailboxes throughout Custer County are doomed to early death, if not from cattle drives, then from vandalism, specifically, drive-by shootings. Our shiny silver mailbox, standing a mile from the house and miles and miles from anywhere else, all but invites gunplay. A new mailbox every year is not in our budget. So at the end of every hunting season Stew plugs the bullet holes with putty to keep out rain.

"You have to walk a mile for your mail, a whole mile?" (My mother is concerned. She loves me. I write to her about everything that does and does not happen on Sawmill Creek.) Well, walking is more what I do on the sidewalks of Main Street. Here I hike the mile to Morgan Creek Road, turn around, and hike back, or I ski or snow-shoe or haul ass on my fat-tired mountain bike. Hey, when you move to the moon you're lucky to have mail delivered at all.

Three times a week, by pickup truck or snowmobile, mail is delivered to the gut-shot mailbox on Morgan Creek Road, not by the postal service, but by a trucking company hired by the postal service, which amounts to very nearly the same thing. Packages are delivered there, too. So we can order things like vegetable seeds, gopher traps, sleeping bags, tents, fly-tying supplies, office supplies, photography supplies, hunting supplies, reloading supplies, leather-making supplies. Just about everything we need. If we had money to burn we could mail order from the Cumberland General Store things we don't really need, but things we really, really want, things like a treadle sewing machine, a windmill, a cast iron sausage stuffer, an oak keg for making beer, a custom-built buggy or a two-seater surrey (we haven't decided which), a wash tub with a hand wringer, and most of all a new wood-burning cookstove. We have it all picked out. A Monarch cookstove. It's a beauty, an heirloom, a work of art in lustrous black enamel and gleaming nickel plate. It has an oven so big Stew could cook up a storm and a warming closet just above that. Like I said we have it all picked out. We just have to wait for our ship to come in. The Monarch costs more money than our savings account earns in a year.

For twenty-five dollars you can mail order a set of house plans from the Cumberland catalog. Just choose a floor plan—the "Cottage," the "Santa Fe," the "Old Home

Place." There are other companies that will sell to you, if you are very rich, a log cabin kit. Here again, just pick out a plan, a chalet, a condo, a castle in the air. Crews will mill your logs at the plant, notch them, assemble them with cranes, disassemble them, then ship them to you with the roof of your choice. Remember Lincoln Logs?

Going into debt wasn't (and still isn't) an option with us. We couldn't afford to mail order as much as an outhouse. We couldn't afford to hire crews or cranes or a generator or a cement mixer, had we wanted to, had it even occurred to us to do so, which it didn't. In fact we had set aside so little money for building the house we often had to settle for lower-priced alternatives when it came to mere appearances. And yet we over-built for structural strength.

Without proper equipment, raising the walls, not to mention the roof, was a harrowing experience, downright life-threatening at times. Without any experience every phase of construction, from the foundation to the roof, was based on inspirational guesswork and what few how-to books we found at the library.

For the most part Stew learned how to build with logs by building a little log cabin on stilts, a "cache" he called it, where we could hang elk and deer meat high above the reach of our fanged neighbors. The mason in Challis taught Stew how to mix cement, how to lay block, how to build a stone floor, and how to build the stone walls behind the stoves. My brother-in-law Harry, a carpenter by trade, taught Stew how to install floor joists and how to connect the fiberglass roof of the greenhouse to the metal roof of the house. The owner of Independent Building Supplies (Salmon, Idaho) taught Stew how to design a steep, snow-shedding metal roof that was economical. And a customer standing at the service counter of Intermountain Lumber (Missoula, Montana) taught Stew how to crown and glue boards together for a ridgepole, thus saving us from having to buy expensive factory-laminated beams.

We saved even more money by shopping outside Challis. Every spring, before we started building, we sent project bids to lumber yards in Salmon, Pocatello, Idaho Falls, and Missoula, where competition between lumber yards was fierce to say the least. But competition or not, most of these lumber yards would not make deliveries to the moon. So we rented a U-haul utility trailer and drove home everything we could, things like boxes of nails, rolls of fiberglass insulation, rolls of tar paper, sacks of lime, sacks of cement, and short lengths of lumber. Loads too long for the trailer or too fragile we had to buy from the few companies that would deliver. Or they

Stew builds our fence

would sort of deliver. The drivers, having mucked their way up muddy Morgan Creek Road, could not be bribed to muck it on up just a little bit further, just another mile to the building site. So everything was lifted off or tilted off the flatbed trucks and stacked along Morgan Creek Road, all those four-by-fours and four-by-sixes and four-by-eights, all those sheets of plywood and sheets of metal roofing and sheets of window glass. It took us five days to shuttle the thousand cinderblocks that would become the foundation for the house.

After we stacked the cinderblocks into four neat units at convenient places around the foundation site, a bunch of chipmunks took up leisurely residence in the blocks, turning them into multi-storied condos. They filled some of the holes in the blocks with nests, then with baby chipmunks, even as Stew was dismantling their condos and mortaring the blocks to the foundation wall. By the time the condos were fully dismantled the baby chipmunks were fully grown and thinking of having babies of their own.

These chipmunks and their cute little tricks barely relieved the tedium of building the foundation walls, masonry work being tedious under the best of conditions. From dawn to dusk, day after day, week after week, month after month, come rain or heat or unexpected company, we worked on that wall. I sifted sand for the mortar, measured the sand into a wheelbarrow, then added measured amounts of lime and cement, then measured amounts of water (Roy hauled the water by buckets from the creek). Chad stirred the mortar in a wheelbarrow with a hoe taller than he was. Roy carried the mortar piled on a palette to Stew seated beside the unfinished wall. With a putty knife Stew buttered the bottoms of each block. With the critical eye of an artist in the throes of creation, he stuck each block to the wall, level and square. When the wall was finished we capped it with a subfloor of fir and covered the subfloor with tar paper to protect it. It goes without saying, you could put into a sardine tin all the fun we had that first building season.

I should mention that our foundation wall was built around a three-foot-deep hole. With a small backhoe borrowed from the Thompson Creek Mine, Stew had dug this hole on weekends while he was employed by the mine. The Custer County building inspector made us dig this hole, a "crawlspace" he called it, so the plumbing inspector could crawl around down there and inspect the plumbing—never mind that indoor plumbing was just one of the modern amenities our cabin wouldn't have. As for the rest of that building code stuff, well, we just skipped it.

Stew, being a person loathed to waste space, gave me this wasted space, a "root cellar" he called it. I was quite unable to tell it from a hole in the ground. Later, when he had more time, he would build me a proper root cellar, something more traditional, something like what they use to have in this country in the time before supermarkets made root cellars obsolete. I have it all planned, my dream root cellar. It will have room to stand up in, lots of shelves, and a door. It will be dug into the north-facing hillside behind the house, conveniently close to the house. Trouble is, it will have to be dug by hand. Shovels. Picks. Pry bars for the boulders. No work for a woman, this kind of digging. Surely someday Stew will find the time. Meanwhile I am still crawling around this crawlspace, this root cellar, this dark airless dungeon.

Being Dropouts from the World of Earn, we were free to sally south that first winter and the second winter (by the third winter we were moved in). That November, before snowfall trapped us, we hitched the trailer to the pickup and headed out with the snow geese. To keep within our budget we camped in campgrounds that charged no fee and we hauled our self-sufficiency along. It never occurred to us to do anything less.

In the back of the pickup, under the fiberglass camper shell, Stew packed six months' worth of food and supplies, stuff like beans, flour, sugar, oats, rice, syrup, vinegar, oil, shampoo, toilet paper, textbooks, and notebook paper. On a plywood platform installed on top of all this, the boys would sleep on foam mattresses.

Also packed in back, or I should say, bolted to the pickup bed, were two metal chests, their drawers, all thirteen of them, filled to capacity with the tools Stew needed to fix the pickup should it break down. You see, first we bought our property. Then to get us there, we bought this used Dodge Ram pickup, a tough truck built for cross-country travel, with enough oomph to cross creeks and climb hills (four on the floor, baby). Although Stew fine-tuned the engine before we headed out, the truck, being over a hundred thousand miles old, was far from trouble free.

Less than a thousand miles into our winter migration, at a freeway rest stop in southern Utah, Stew had to dive into his magic toolbox to change one of the trailer's tires, it having developed an ominous bubble the size of a baseball. Then he noticed how both trailer tires, both spanking new trailer tires, were worn to their cords. He decided to check out the trailer's axle, something he should have done before we bought the trailer secondhand from Rancher-the-name-doesn't-matter. And guess what he found? The axle was bent, so bent it was unsafe to travel even a mile further.

Stew said we would have to camp. Camp? Where? Right here at this rest stop. And we did camp, for two days, while Stew pulled off the trailer's axle and straightened it with a pry bar, a cheater pipe, a come-along, a sledge hammer, two hydraulic jacks, and forty feet of chain. Then we bought two new spanking-new trailer tires. We were on our way again, two tons of house hurtling behind us.

The rest of that first winter we spent in Arizona, camping on the beaches of Roosevelt Lake, Apache Lake, and the many backwater lakes of the Colorado River. Stands of paloverde and cottonwoods shaded the camp table where the boys pored over their textbooks from the time after breakfast until sometime after lunch. Then we would all have a heckuva swell time swimming, fishing, catching crawdads for dinner, and just generally enjoying our family life, our solitude. We all grew brown and strong with swimming and fat on fried catfish and bass. Each beach we found seemed better than the last, and always we wanted to stay after our two-week limit was up, and always the BLM rangers made us move on.

The next winter we went to California, strayed into the vast public domain west of Blythe. There is a campground here called Coon Hollow administered as a "Long Term Visitor Area," meaning, the BLM rangers don't make you move on. For only twenty-five dollars we got to stay the entire winter. We had water from a well, a picnic table, a barbecue pit, a pit toilet, garbage collection, and a campground host to control the riffraff that came every holiday weekend to party in the great outdoors.

But we had no lake for fishing and swimming. We had no solitude, no family life, or not much of a family life anyway, the boys having grown older, more outward, more independent. But this isn't to say we didn't have good times there, too.

Through this preposterously blooming wasteland of sand, I would hike every day after school, sometimes with Roy, more often alone. I hiked to the low rocky hills where the wind shifted sand into fans and desert lilies stood waist-high and smelling for all the world like Easter morning.

Roy, a quiet daydreaming boy, preferred his own company to that of others. As a budding biologist he liked to knock around the sandy washes that occasional thunderstorms turned into raging rivers of mud, sticks, and foam. A few days after such a storm, grasses grew in clumpy patches and wild burros came out of hiding to graze, and just for the fun of it, to gallop around. Tortoises, caked with mud, came out of their dens, plugging along, going nowhere it seemed, so burdened were they by their hard heavy housing. There were high-stepping tarantulas and hunting lizards large and small, Roy learned them all by species, by name. Whiptails, zebra tails, iguanas. He learned to read animal tracks, the illiterate scribbles made by pocket mice and kangaroo rats and the strange marks made by the sidewinders that hunted them. He watched squadrons of turkey vultures wheeling wide-winged over-head, waiting for something to die, always waiting for something to die, waiting in vain it would seem, the desert was so green and alive. In these washes Roy learned more than all his textbooks could ever hope to teach.

Most of the time after school, Stew spent in camp, working on the table cleared of textbooks. Ever the archi-tect he fine-tuned his house plans, sketching in where the stoves would go, the cupboards and counters, the walk-in pantry with its wide sturdy shelves and its ladder access-ing the loft. Yet even as he was preparing for the future (the future being the next building season on Sawmill Creek), he was living, in every sense of the word, in the present, in the warm sun-shiny desert. So when he wasn't sitting with his how-to books borrowed from the Blythe Library, or sitting with his guitar, he was sitting with our fellow campers, the snowbird retirees for whom sitting and talking were principal recreation.

Come sundown, Stew started searching the camp-ground, tracking down Chad (for whom sitting and talking were also principal recreation). Chad, as gregarious as Roy was shy, spent all his afternoons calling door-to-door on his many surrogate grandparents. You see, at age nine Chad was a free-flowing talker. He played fast and loose with the truth when he wanted to bring attention to himself, to his plight. Which was? Well, he described himself as poor, needy, underprivileged, disadvantaged, deprived of all the good things in life, deprived by his parents' poverty. Our trailer, our sad battered tin box, gave proof, parked as it was among these fancy Airstreams, Winnebagos, and Prowlers, most of them equipped with solar panels, satel-lite dishes, hot tubs, microwave ovens, and killer sound systems.

When at last Chad came home, with chocolate-smeared mouth and sickening-sweet breath, we were well into dinner. Of course, being late was never his fault, he always had two or three stories ready to roll. It was Bert's fault or Chester's fault or Homer's fault, as if he had been forced to watch their televisions (we didn't have a television, we didn't need a television, Chad was entertainment enough). It was also never his fault that he wasn't hungry for dinner. It was Bertha's fault or Ethel's fault or Em's fault, as if he had been forced to snack so he wouldn't starve to death before dinner (Chad would starve to death a dozen times before dinner). Stew and I could see clearly just how Chad spent his afternoons playing on the sympathy of these grandmothers, sitting and telling them about us, us old food fogies, how we never let him have sweets, always made him eat boring beans and oatmeal and all that yucky fiber junk. What else, we wondered, did Chad tell them about us? What the hell else, real or imagined?

In early March when dozens of diamondback rattlesnakes (aka *coon*tails) came snaking out their dens to coil up in the shade of Coon Hollow Campground, all Chad's surrogate grandparents cranked in their candy-striped awnings, packed up their poodles, their plastic lawns and plastic picket fences, and got the holy heck out of the desert. By mid April we were completely alone and as sun-puckered as the prickly pear cactus. With the snakes we panted in the hundred-degree shade, what little shade there was in all that sun. That sun. Was it the same sun, do you suppose, that shines on central Idaho? Turned out it wasn't but we headed home anyway.

Homeward bound we merged with the stream of tail lights on the interstates. We clipped along the long lonesome length of U.S. 93, running north, running back through time, back through spring and directly into winter. We turned up Morgan Creek Road and came to rest at the mouth of Sawmill Creek, the truck stuck in snow, interred to the tailpipe in snow. Having to camp here did not disturb us in the least. It wasn't so much an inconvenience as it was a chance to wind down, to decompress from all that driving, all that pushing rushing traffic. After spending a few days resting, then a few more days hacking down snowdrifts in the driveway, Stew chained up the truck and horsed us home. If all went as planned during this (our second) building season, we would have the log walls up and the roof on before we had to go south again.

We chose logs for walls, over stones, over conventional lumber, over whatever else was available we never even thought to ask, because log walls would stand up remarkable well to earthquakes and insulate just as well in forty-below cold. Only a log cabin would look right on Sawmill Creek. It would stand as a romantic emblem of the past, an embodiment of those wonderful virtues of the past, namely, simplicity, practicality, economy, endurance, and homey warmth.

At first we planned to go into the surrounding forests and get our own logs. We figured out how we'd just get a permit from the Challis Ranger District, won't cost us hardly a thing, then thin out those stands of straight tall lodgepole pines (in those days they were in bad need of thinning). But what we didn't get figured out was where to rent a logging truck, a skidder, and a bulldozer. So much for do-it-yourself logging.

As it turned out we hired Logger Larry, a local man, who cut our timbers, squared them off on two sides for a better fit, and delivered them to us for under two thousand dollars—paid in advance. Or he sort of delivered them. He made it up Morgan Creek Road alright, with his logging truck and a long flatbed trailer in tow, both truck and trailer heaped high and heavy with logs. He made it up the driveway alright, and across the culvert we had just installed to bridge the creek-crossing below the building site. Our plans were to have the hydraulic boom on the logging truck unload the logs onto a set of cribs set up beside the foundation wall. Well plans ran amuck, literally. The logging truck couldn't pull the steep far end of the driveway, it was slick from a recent rain. So Larry slid the truck back down, then spun all the mud off the culvert trying to grab for traction, trying to move forward again. The culvert collapsed, caved in on itself, causing Larry to throw up his hands. He backed the truck and trailer into the meadow, and there, beside the boys' tent, he unloaded the logs, piled them going every which way like jackstraws. How we would get them to the building site wasn't his problem. What did he care. He was already paid.

Stew, ever the clever one, the one to see a challenge where I see defeat, always confident in himself and in his tools, fixed the culvert like he fixed the trailer's axle and with pretty much the same set of tools. Then with chains, ropes, pulleys, snatch blocks, and two leftover fence poles, he built a crane and mounted it to the back of the pickup bed. This crane was a fairly half-assed setup, Stew would be the first to admit it. But it worked. With it we towed each log to the building site, then later, lifted the logs up the walls of the house, then much later, lifted the ridgepole to the top of the house. In fact this crane worked so well we use it today for all kinds of things.

By the time we were ready to raise the walls, the logs, having been peeled and laid crisscrossed on the cribs, had done most of their drying and shrinking. One by one Roy and I carried the logs from the cribs to a set of sawhorses. Here Stew, using his chainsaw, cut the logs into measured length, notched their corner ends, and fitted their unnotched ends together. Then we stacked the logs tier upon tier, spiked them into place, and fastened them with

dowels to the logs underneath. This part went surprisingly well thanks to weeks of pleasant weather and a run of
good luck.

The doors and windows Stew had made beforehand
went up with the log walls. Their frames were keyed into
place not nailed, so when the logs continued to dry and
shrink over the years the frames didn't create wall gaps
even though the walls shrank over an inch.

Installing the windows did not go as well as it could
have. For the first time, but not the last time, the weather
turned on us. Quite suddenly. Luck left us. Abruptly.

It had been an uncommonly lovely morning, cool and
sunny, a few little summer clouds, not even the barest sug-
gestion of a breeze, the perfect morning to install windows.
And by noon two windows had been installed, or sort of
installed. They sat perched on the two kitchen walls, four
logs high, propped there by poles until the next course of
logs would hold them in tight. A seven-foot-long picture
window, wrapped in rope, dangled from the crude crane en
route to the living room wall. You see what's coming don't
you? Well we didn't, not at first. No one saw the black
clouds forming, curdling in the southern sky. But we all
heard the demented howl of the wind, saw the wind whipping a path through the firs, bending low their tops, tear-
ing off their leaves and arms, churning this debris of
leaves and twigs, dust and pollen, confused insects and
frazzled birds, this awful wind sucking up everything,
spinning it to eternity, coming our way in boisterous
cyclonic swirls.

In just moments this twister, this tornado, whatever
the heck it was, reached us. Had we enough time to think
about what to do I doubt there was much else we could
have done to save all the windows. With the wind fully
upon us Chad and I stood hanging on for dear life to the
picture window wildly swinging, straining for flight like a

Roy and Stew install the ceiling.

kite. Stew stood hanging on to the nearest kitchen window, shouldering it as the wind tried to tear it away, as Roy ran, ran hard, toward the farthest kitchen window. A shout from Stew, and crash! over went the window, hitting the floor—smash! to tinkling glass. Quite suddenly, quite dramatically, wall-raising came to a stop. For two weeks we waited for a new pane of glass to be cut, delivered, and installed inside its frame.

A few weeks after that, with windows and doors permanently in place, with walls eleven logs high and only one more course of logs to go, luck left us again. I was holding the ladder for Stew, firmly, by the legs. He was standing on the top step, balanced touch-and-go. He had shucked his shirt. It was August and hot. His hands were full of tools. He was hammering in log spikes. You see what's coming don't you? A horsefly. A bloodthirsty beast with a bite so vicious a hypo to the backside is but a kiss in comparison. Soft as a feather it landed right smack in the middle of Stew's back, right where he couldn't have reached it had he felt it, which he didn't, and had his hands been empty, which they weren't. Then he did feel it and his hands were quite suddenly empty and his arms were flailing the air. I heard a horrid strangled croak and a strange soprano yelp. Helplessly I watched Stew flailing, flailing the air, falling, falling to the ground. There was a thud, silence, then a groan. Stew's sprained ankle idled us for another week. I am not making this up. I do not make things up. I can't make things up. I would write novels and make big money if I could.

What happened just days after the final log course was in place had more to do with stupidity than bad luck. Stew and I were about to install four tie-logs, thirty-footers that would span the width of the house and strengthen the entire structure. My job was easy. While Stew rolled the first log across the wall I was supposed to stand there pointing my finger to the black dot on the wall where the notched-end of the tie-log would drop into place. I watched the log roll. I watched the notched-end drop smashing into place, right where it was supposed to, right on the black dot, and GAAAK! right on my finger. Pain tore through me. A mess of my own red blood was smeared on the log, splattered on the floor, and still it was pumping out. With great calmness and presence of mind I ran screaming to Stew, scaring heck out of both of us. Then my finger was being wrapped with a sanitary napkin to stop the bleeding. I was being calmed and soothed. It's not as bad as it looks. It's not as bad as it looks. Omigod, yes it is, yes it is. It's bad, it's bad. My finger, or what used to be my finger, the index finger of my right hand, the finger I use most, the finger I need most, was now a raw hash-mash of bloody meat. How did it happen? Stew wanted to know. I didn't know. I just didn't know. I guess I forgot to move my finger out of the way. I had hurt myself by being stupid. But Stew did not hurt me again with angry scolding. This is not his style, not now, not then, even when we could ill afford the time, not to mention the money, it would take to fix my finger, if in fact my finger could be fixed at all.

In less than twenty minutes we were at the first-aid station in Challis. The doctor sprinkled Novocaine on my wound and took more stitches than I thought my finger had in it. He wrapped my finger in yards of gauze, made of my finger a small white club, and sent me home with a prescription to kill the pain that would be my life when the Novocaine wore off. And he made me promise to use a ruler to point out the rest of the black dots, which is what I most certainly would do.

Stupidity, both my stupidity and Stew's, led to another needless injury. It's hard to see it any other way. In this case the victim was our dog Oggy, a mixed breed we had adopted after the malamute pup grew up and ran away. Oggy was black. His markings were tan and perfect. He watched the world through big brown eyes. He was my dog, my friend when I had no other, my fishing buddy when the boys were at school and Stew was at work. Together, on cold winter mornings, Oggy and I worked over stretches of stream likely to hold sleeping steelhead. I'll try to tell this in a level voice, without emotions.

Oggy's accident happened toward the end of August. With all the delays, we were feeling rushed to get the cabin closed in before we had to head south again. Building materials for the roof, having been delivered months ago, were spread out in an orderly manner on cribs arranged in the meadow. There was stainless-steel stovepipe and sheet metal for the roof and lumber for the roof and lumber for the ceiling and lumber for the gable ends. Still we needed more lumber, more two-by-fours, before we could begin raising the roof. Also we needed to go to the market, the library, the launderette. Trying to save time we made what should have been two trips to town into one. Getting ready to drive home, we found no room in the cab for Oggy. With grave misgivings, with bells going off in our heads, we loaded him into the open bed of the pickup piled high with lumber. Stew said he would drive slowly. And he did. Then he swerved to miss a rock slide and Oggy shot overboard, landing in a ditch he couldn't climb out of. His right hind leg, the bone shattered beyond repair, had to be amputated by the vet.

For the next six years Oggy got around on three legs with all his former agility and speed. But when he turned ten–seventy in human terms, if every year of a dog's age is approximately seven years in human terms–his lone hind leg became stiff and sore from bearing all the weight. His biting end became more active than his wagging end. On some of our walks Stew had to carry him home, muzzled, one arm under his chest, the other under his belly, a heavy awkward armful. One winter, pain became the sum of Oggy's life.

It had to be done, had to! Stew's overtones carried the quality of despair. He had decided he didn't want to make any heroic efforts to keep Oggy going. Under the circumstances this is what I would have wanted done to me, but not on a frigid December morning, not that there's ever good weather for euthanizing your dog. Just talking about this, just thinking about it, still comes hard to us even today, as if Oggy were a brand-new wound, as if sorrow had fists to pound our hearts. We still feel such regret and guilt. Oggy was so full of affection for us. That's what made it so hard. He trusted Stew, suspected nothing, being used to Stew carrying a gun along on their walks. It took Stew hours to find a good spot, at least that's how long it was before I heard the shot that sent a bullet into Oggy's brain. Believe me, time will never heal this one.

If nothing else Oggy's tragedy taught us to slow down. The huge looming project of raising the roof would be dangerous enough. The roof had to be high, high enough to make headroom for the loft, and steep, steep enough to slide off the heavy winter snow.

By some combination of cussedness and miracle we managed to raise the ridgepole in four separate sections (this beam spans the length of the house, overhanging the kitchen wall on the east and the porch on the west). With ropes we lifted the first section into place. Easy does it. It was up. Using the crude crane Stew cranked the second section into place, or almost into place. He ran out of reach a foot short. I choose not to remember how he climbed the crane, wobbled to the very top of it, then lifted the heavy beam above his head, held it there, jerked it, cursed it, bolted it in place. Working without a net he pulled the same stunts until the entire assembly was up and bolted in. Then something downright uncanny happened. A male mountain bluebird flew in from nowhere, landed on the west end of the ridgepole, and claimed it for a stage. From here, for the next seven years, he flaunted his beauty, his remarkable blueness. It wasn't so far-fetched to believe his arrival was a good omen. We were ready for some good luck.

I should mention that Stew designed the ridgepole in such a way that it allows the entire roof to settle evenly, without sagging, as the log walls continue to shrink over the years. Underneath the floor the two support posts holding up the ridgepole are bolted to two metal plates supported, in turn, by two jacks (Stew built these jacks with a rented welder.) Once a year, or whenever he has to, and only when he has to, Stew lowers himself through the hatchway in the pantry, crawls around in the gloom of the crawlspace-cum-root-cellar, and lowers the jacks to compensate for wall shrinkage.

After raising the ridgepole Stew and I raised the ribs of the roof, the rafters, eighteen-foot-long boards, sixty of them. While barn swallows swirled around, chattering about future nesting sites, I straddled the top log of the wall and hugged tight the bottom end of each rafter so it wouldn't slide to the ground. High overhead Stew stood on a ladder-like affair and bolted his end of the board to the ridgepole. For weeks we worked like this, moving slowly across the wall from east to west, as slowly the sun moved across the sky from east to west and left the sky in a glory of red. One afternoon lightning bolts moved from west to east, announcing the storm that would soaked us before Stew finally called "QUIT!"

After the ridgepole, after the rafters, Stew and I stood at a deadly height on a catwalk supported by the tie-logs. Stew stapled the plastic vapor barrier to the underside of each set of rafters while I held the plastic in place, cranking my head ceilingward, then downward to refill the staple gun. I kept noticing the narrowness of the catwalk and the ground spinning dizzily far below me, so far below it would have scared even the daring young man on the flying trapeze. I grew dizzier. I yelled at Roy to come take my place.

With the vapor barrier installed Stew and Roy stood on the catwalk nailing in the ceiling and gable ends. A week later Stew stood alone on top of the rafters while his ground crew roped up to him thick yellow rolls of insulation, then full-size sheets of plywood, then rolls of tarpaper, then long lengths of sheet-metal roofing. For two weeks Stew spent most of his daylight hours alone, staggering toward the peak of the roof, straddling the space between two adjacent rafters, the soles of his tennis shoes gripping each rafter edge. His left hand held the rope that kept him from falling while his right hand unrolled insulation or nailed down plywood or tacked down tarpaper. Then with his left hand clutching his lifeline and the holding-handle of the drill and his right hand turning the turning-handle of the drill, he screwed the metal roofing to the plywood with well over a thousand screws. For two weeks I maintained a helpless vigil on the ground while Stew, the essence of my existence, my third and final husband, did his high-wire act, juggling his lifeline, a drill, a hammer, nails, tacks, screws (I would not have been surprised to see him cartwheeling across the peak). At best a fall would result in broken bones, at worse, sure and sudden death.

Raising the roof went without mishap because of Stew's agility and his cautious unhurried paced (no doubt having the blue hope perched on the ridgepole helped). How we ended up right on schedule still puzzles me though. See, Stew usually supposes he can get something done in less time than it actually takes him. He is always full of errant enthusiasm. He creates such suspense he arouses me to states of worry. Obviously this wasn't the case here. By the time snow began powdering the hillsides around us the two chimneys had been installed and we were packing for our winter migration.

I should mention that Stew built the chimneys using only expensive stainless steel stovepipe. It doesn't rust. And it's designed to prevent soot from accumulating, the accumulation of soot being the major cause of chimney fires according to the Challis Volunteer Fire Department. Taking fire prevention another step Stew strapped the chimneys to the roof with steel braces so they wouldn't topple during roof avalanches.

We have two chimneys poking out the roof. The one over the living room vents our airtight wood-burning Earth Stove, a heating stove we bought on sale while living in Challis. The stove has a flat top wide enough to hold three tea kettles at one time, plus a chili cooker, plus (this is a real squeeze) the caldron Stew uses to mash barley for his beer.

The chimney over the kitchen vents the old cookstove

we bought for a hundred bucks from a friend. We needed something to get us by until something better came along. We were damn lucky to get it, having been consistently outbid by antique dealers on every old wood-burning cookstove. Unfortunately this one had been grossly abused. The porcelain was gashed, the oven corroded, the chrome trim scabbed with rust, the top rusted, scarred, and stained, the sides riddled with rusty bullet holes. Nevertheless, we love it, Stew loves it, loves cooking on it, wouldn't part with it even if something better came along (Monarchs excepted). Who wouldn't love it? It fries venison burgers to perfection and bakes bread golden brown.

Our second winter in the desert would be our last winter in the desert if all went well, if all went as planned. Again, in late April, we returned to Sawmill Creek, with the bluebirds and kinglets, the bluebells and buttercups. Again, from the sidelines, we would watch spring become summer become fall, at which point we would be ready to move in, if all went well, if all went as planned.

Plumbing, our first project that spring, was so back-woods basic it should have been a cinch to install. Some of it was. But without power tools, without a cement mixer, without a backhoe, some of it wasn't.

We didn't want anything as complex as drain lines and a leach field. So, like in the good old days, waste water from the kitchen sink and the bathroom sink simply drains into five-gallon plastic buckets we dump into the slop hole out back. Of course my mother doesn't think this is so charmingly rustic. She thinks it's downright uncivilized. She's right.

On the plus side we don't have to fight frozen sewage in this near-Arctic climate. We don't have to fight frozen water lines either. We don't have water lines. We don't have a pressure tank or a well or a pump or a generator, all of which we would have had to install had we wanted running water in the house, which, in case you are wondering, we did not, as uncivilized as that might sound.

Consequently, without running water, we have no modern conveniences, no modern necessities. No washing machine. No dishwasher. No shower. No flush toilet. No matter, I had told Stew when we were planning the plumbing. Like the pioneers I would rough it. I could get used to a washboard and tub, a dishrag and sink, a Saturday night bath, an outhouse. Well hold on a minute. An outhouse? When it rains? When it's forty below zero? When it's dark and black widow spiders are lurking about? Don't you think an outhouse is going a bit too far back into the good old days?

The comforts of humankind are vitally important, mine included. And like everyone, when I want something, I'm not above sniveling or bitching or bootlicking, should it come to that. With the outhouse it came to that before my Sugarbear agreed to build an outhouse indoors, or not an outhouse exactly, but a waterless composting toilet, something that operates much like a compost pile in the garden. Through a natural combination of heat and oxygen bacteria break down human wastes and organic kitchen scraps into humus, a dark organic material. This humas is so free of pathogens, when we remove it from the tank every two years or so, we dig it directly into the vegetable beds.

Stew designed the tank of our composting toilet after the Clivus Multrum, the most popular, trouble-free model on the market, a model, by the way, that costs thousands of dollars. Before raising the walls of the house, Stew had built our tank out of sheets of plywood and two-by-fours. He had driven the tank to a camper shell factory in Pocatello where it was lined with fiberglass. On the freeway, the cars zipping by would brake all of a sudden, and the drivers would lean far out their windows and gawked at this . . . this . . . squarish, tallish, wooden . . . thing. Back home, using the crude crane, Stew lifted the tank out of the truck and into the mini-basement designed especially for the tank (and built inside the walls of the foundation).

Composting toilets are not the rustic privy-like products my mother might imagine. They look like modern flush toilets. The tanks below ground are, of course, hidden from view. The commodes above ground are sold in a range of beautiful colors and designs to match any home decor. Our commode, more beautiful than anything you could buy, matches our bathroom walls, as well it should, having been built out of scrap lumber left over from building those walls. Stew lipped the lid of this commode with weather stripping. When not in use this lid clamps down and seals tightly so gasses and odors don't rise into the bathroom. Instead they rise through a long length of stovepipe extending from the tank to the roof and out, where they vanish into the huge blue beyond.

After our custom crapper was installed, we tossed into the tank several bucketfuls of dirt dug from the creek bank, dirt full of the microbes needed to get the composting action going. On top of this dirt we added—well, we just started using the toilet. And it worked fine. For a year or so.

The problems with all composting toilets, manufactured or otherwise, come during the first year or two of use. This is the breaking in period when adjustments must be made, when all kinds of kinks must be worked out. For my mother's sake I'll try to handle this matter as delicately as I can.

Year one: Unbeknownst to us, for months, hoards of flies from the huge blue beyond had been flying down the stovepipe and into the tank where they feasted and frolicked in our feces. Whenever the toilet lid was opened, out buzzed the flies, zzzzzt, covered from feeler to foot with potentially dangerous pathogens. Out the bathroom door they flew and into the kitchen where food was always being prepared.

Hitting the books again–he read them all–Stew slogged his way through the swamp of data on composting toilets until he found a paragraph that all but screamed, "Screen the top of the exhaust pipe." He did, and in short order we were free of flies. We were ready for problem number two when it came around.

Year two: Out the opened toilet lid came the putrid smell of rot. Hitting the books again Stew read, ever so carefully this time, how the balance between air and moisture in the composting process is a delicate thing, how excessive urine, like that produced by heavy coffee drinkers such as ourselves, can pool at the bottom of the tank. This pooling of urine, or any liquid for that matter, encourages anaerobic composting (meaning, without oxygen), the same kind of composting that occurs in swamps, cesspools, and at the bottom of garbage cans that haven't been emptied in a while. Before our tank would return to odorless aerobic composting (with oxygen), this excess liquid had to be removed.

First, Stew had the boys dig a deep hole at the far end of the yard. Then he had me stand beside the toilet while he stood below me under the hatched access in the bathroom floor, beside the clean-out hatch of the tank. For over an hour he handed up to me buckets and buckets of–well, you can imagine! Ever so carefully so as not to slop across the floor I carried each bucket out the door and dumped it into the hole. When the tank was empty the boys filled the hole with dirt. Through all this, rubber gloves kept things sanitary. Gas masks would have been nice.

As the books point out liquid build-up is an ongoing problem in cold climates. The only heat for our tank comes via PVC pipes that capture the warm air beside the Earth Stove. Obviously this isn't enough heat to evaporate all that urine, even had we decided to eliminate coffee from our mornings. What we decided to eliminate was urine from our tank. Now our night waters flow into a modern-day chamber pot, a Port-o-Potty as you might know it, which is dumped daily into the outhouse out back. Now that the problems have been worked out, I can say this about our composting toilet. My happiness depends on it.

Before I say anything more about our backwoods plumbing I would like to say something to console my mother who I have surely, thoroughly shamed, and who I will no doubt shame again. Mom, I want you to know that our urine is clean. Unlike feces, our urine, your urine, the urine of all healthy people, is free of pathogens. It's freer of germs than a mother's kiss. Around the world people in the millions drink their urine, yes, they drink it, for medicinal purposes. By the way it's supposed to taste like warm beer, however I'm not qualified to pronounce on this.

How we bathe is likewise semi-civilized although originally plans called for something else. What we had in mind was a bathtub made of cast iron and porcelain, something standing on paws, enthroned on a platform so the used bath water could drain into a slop bucket.

Before we even bought a bathtub, before we even looked into buying a bathtub, Stew built the platform at one corner of two bathroom walls, flush with the walls. In order to access the slop bucket he cut a door into the side of the platform. To hide the bucket, I made a curtain for the door (and while I had needle in hand, a curtain for the bathroom window) using yards of this lovely drapery material I paid too much for at the store. I also splurged on eight fluffy bath towels, hand towels, washcloths, hand-woven hardwood baskets to hold them all, and a beautiful dish of hammered brass to hold the soap, everything to be nicely arranged beside the tub.

We let our fingers do the walking through the pages of Cumberland's catalog. We came to bathtubs. Horrors! What we had in mind, what we had built the platform for, cost well over two thousand dollars. There was shipping, too. Or rather there wasn't shipping. It was too heavy for UPS and too big for the mailmobile. We let our fingers walk on until we came to something cheaper, lots cheaper, real cheap. What we bought was a tank made of galvanized tin, the kind used for watering cattle.

We still use the stock-watering tank, it worked that well. It's so lightweight, in winter we carry it from the cold bathroom to the kitchen where it's warm beside the stove or to the greenhouse where it's even warmer with all that sun pouring unobstructed through the panes. In summer we install it more or less permanently directly under the sun, between the rhubarb bed and the strawberry patch. There I sink into the bath water until it is shoulder high. When I emerge I'm as wrinkled as a morel mushroom.

In winter the water we need for bathing, cooking, washing dishes, washing clothes, and washing everything else comes from five-gallon buckets Stew fills every morning from a hole chopped in the creek ice. In spring, summer, and fall our hydraulic ram pump frees him from this chore.

The ram, an invention over two centuries old, uses a mass of moving water to lift a smaller amount of water far higher than its source — in our case fifty feet, give or take. Some people actually understand how the ram does this, how it works. Then there are the rest of us mechanical Neanderthals. Not only do I not understand these things, I do not care to understand these things I do not understand.

I don't know how the ram works but it does work, and

with very little maintenance, just a few simple adjustments here and there once or twice a season. It only
breaks when something gets pounded too hard.

If you have the money you can buy a ram. We didn't
have the money so Stew built ours using this plan he
found in an old issue of *Mother Earth News* and scaling it
down in size, Sawmill Creek being such a small creek compared to *Mother's* creek. At the hardware store he bought
lots of pipes, check valves, and fittings, then stuck everything together according to plan.

In milder climates, *Mother* points out, rams operate
indefinitely given the uninterrupted energy source of running water. Although Sawmill Creek runs all winter under
the ice, our ram doesn't run at all. As I understand it the
water in the diversion dam, in the pipes, and in the ram
itself would freeze and everything would crack and break
if Stew didn't shut it down before winter comes nipping
along.

Sawmill Creek roars with runoff in May. In August it's
barely deep enough to float a fish. In September it can't
even keep its whole length running. Behind our property
and in front, it dwindles to a damp cattle-gutted gully, a
foul rope of mud.

I can't explain why, even in September, the creek con-
tinues to flow across our property, through the tall grasses and sedges, the willows and alders, into the diversion
dam, into the pump, then up, up, up the hillside through
underground pipes to a manifold of faucets at the edge of
our front yard. The first of these three faucets is connected to another underground pipeline. This one fills the
three-hundred-gallon concrete tank Stew built into the
hillside above the house, a tank that supplies water under
pressure to the garden. The second faucet is connected to
a short length of garden hose which in turn is connected to
a spigot screwed to the outside wall of the greenhouse

which in turn is connected to assorted fittings and pipes which in turn are connected to one or the other fifty-five gallon plastic barrels mounted inside the greenhouse. A pitcher pump bolted to the kitchen counter delivers drinking water from the barrels to the sink, drinking water somewhat filtered, much less animated. The third faucet isn't connected to anything yet. Given enough time Stew will come up with something.

Plumbing installed, we turned our collective energies to installing the floor in the loft. As usual building materials were make-do where it didn't matter. As always construction was slow using tools that didn't plug in—hammers, saws, chisels, rasps, sanding blocks, drawknife, hand drill, brace and bit. Some tools, by the way, came from junk stores and auctions. Some tools were made by Stew. He's really good at that kind of thing, fabricating tools, puzzling things out. According to Stew, there is little he cannot do, and I, for one, am very impressed. He seems to have a lot of what I have only a little of.

One tool Stew made was the scribe he needed to mark notches on the logs (he couldn't find one anywhere). First he took a block of wood and carved something that looked like a compass. Then he drilled a hole in its handle and inserted a black marking pen. Then he glued a bull's-eye level to the top. Did it work? Of course it did. Child's play. Like I said, Stew is good.

Another tool Stew made was the transit he needed to line up the fence posts, to level the lot, and to level the walls of the foundation. Transits are expensive. Ours wasn't. Stew took the tripod off my camera and the spotting scope off his rifle. Using a rented welder he made a frame with some bolts and pieces of steel. He screwed my tripod to the bottom of this frame and his rifle scope to the top. Yes this worked, too. Stew's quite a guy!

Power tools scream. Hand tools whisper. Chip-chip-

chip went Stew's chisel, chopping mortises and tendons out of the floor joists, or I should say, out of the leftover house logs that served as floor joists for the loft. Whack-whack-whack went his hammer, nailing tongue-and-groove boards over the joists. Through all this what little noise Stew made didn't seem to disturb the barn swallows nesting beneath the roof. Not at first anyway. But the closer he came to their nest, the more often they flew away in alarm. We were afraid they would abandon the nest entirely in which case we would have to raise their babies as our own, keep them warm, keep them clean, keep them safe, keep them fed, these five ugly featherless hatchlings all sprawled across each other, their beaks gaping in hunger. Having created this nesting site in the first place we now had the unwanted responsibility of ensuring that the nestlings were fledged, no matter what it would do to our building schedule. To heck with our schedule.

Stew climbed down from the loft, leaving a gap in the floor long and wide, a gap that gaped for over three weeks, which was how long it took those damn hatchlings to fledge. Needless to say the loft got no balustrade that year, or the next year, what with this, that, and the other thing. For over three years the trees for the balustrade lay exposed in our yard where anyone could just walk by and see them. This wasn't too cool. We had poached these trees from the nearby forests, a few trees at a time, hidden under the stacks of firewood we did have a permit to cut. Later on we poached more skinny trees when we needed a railing for our porch and more when we needed borders for our gravel pathways and still more when we needed borders for our raised vegetable beds.

Poaching forest products was easy back then, everybody did it, nobody got caught. So when we finished the loft floor we drove to the nearby talus slopes and poached us some slate, slid whole slabs of it down and hauled it home hidden under the pickup's camper shell.

I arranged these slabs of slate into two giant jigsaw puzzles that Stew mortared, a slab at a time, to two cinderblock walls built beforehand, one behind the Earth Stove and one behind the cookstove. With more slate he made mantels, not to display collections of foolish breakable things, but to display rocks, fossils, petrified wood, and animal skulls the boys were wont to drag home. Then we went back to the slopes to slide down more slate for the floors in the bathroom and kitchen.

Before deciding what kind of floors we wanted downstairs we had researched our options. What worked in the olden days and the not-so-olden days? What didn't?

In the beginning there was dirt. Dirt was free and it made a firm floor that soaked up spills rather conveniently. But dirt was out of the question because our subfloor was already installed, and, well, because dirt is dirty.

Then there was linoleum. It was cheap. But linoleum was out because the salesman couldn't guarantee the glues in it would stand up to severe cold, and, well, because linoleum is linoleum. Carpeting was out because we wouldn't have electricity to run a Hoover. So for the kitchen and bathroom, things sort of narrowed down to slate.

First we poured cement floors in the kitchen and bathroom. While waiting for the cement to season I sorted through stacks and stacks of slate, discarding the broken slabs, the slabs too thin, too wavy on top, too beveled at the edges. I arranged the rest into jigsaw puzzles Stew mortared and pressed to the cement floors. After he applied two coats of epoxy the slate in the floors glistened like it had glistened on the slopes after a rain. They're beautiful, these slate floors, these fields of stonework, these collages of polygons in rusty oranges, clay grays, and moss greens, each polygon etched with designs, like lichen.

But for the living room we didn't want slate. It was too cold. We wanted something more like what you see in those slick decorating magazines, a hardwood floor, a sheeny showroom floor. Well why not?

There were lots of reasons why we didn't install a hardwood floor, most of those reasons having to do with expense, a hardwood floor being expensive, beyond our budget, we had looked into it. And being expensive these floors have to be protected with a finish (varnish, shellac, acrylic, what have you). And the finish can only be applied after the floor has been sanded, properly sanded. That's the rub. To do the job properly you need a drum sander, a noisy dangerous wood-eating monster that has to be kept moving at all times. If stopped for even a fraction of a second the sander can leave burn marks and depressions in the floor. Rumors have it that a rental unit in the hands of a novice can ruin a wood floor. These rumors are only partly true. Professionals can ruin a floor with one too. Of course as novices go Stew has way more skill than most. He's a marvel of a man and I had no doubt he could do something like this, something very hard and very dangerous, very well. But if he screwed up, if he screwed up, well, we couldn't afford a new floor. And with that drum sander the odds that he would screw up were greater than the odds that he wouldn't.

There's only one good thing I can say about the fir floor we did install. It was cheap. Nevertheless, it should have been sanded and varnished. The big braided rug that Sears sent doesn't come close to covering up the scuffs and scars and stains left by the years and the boys and the dogs. Without a Hoover this rug isn't all that easy to clean. Stew and I have to roll it up and haul it, heavy as a house log, across the yard to the clothesline. With a one-two-three we heave it. With brooms we soundly thrash it.

We don't have a Hoover because the nearest power line is fifteen miles away. Connecting the cabin to the electrical grid was never under consideration. A generator was ruled out because of the noise, the annoying drone. Solar and wind power were better options but for us, Hoovers aside, living without electricity was the best.

But we wanted lights for our long winter nights, nothing fancy, just glass globes unadorned, fueled with propane. Stew mounted over a dozen of them to the ridgepole supports and to the walls, some lights in pairs where more light was needed. With copper tubing he connected the lights to a propane tank installed outdoors. Propane gives these lights a clean odorless glow for under sixty dollars a year.

Now it was Halloween and flocks of snow geese were flying overhead, heading south without us. Stew had finished framing the greenhouse. He still had to roof it with fiberglass, wall it in with window glass, and make a door before we could move out of the trailer and into the house.

Of all the rooms in the house the greenhouse is my favorite. I live in it as if it were the main room of the house and the living room and kitchen were only annexed, only tacked on as an afterthought. In spring and summer this glassy enclave is my office where I type stories all morning on a huge wooden table surrounded by sunlight and warmth and pots of green growing plants. In winter it is my sun-drenched spa where I thaw my bones and tan my hide. In fall I spread willow mats across the long narrow shelf and dry cabbage leaves, peas, and sliced root vegetables. In spring I dry wild mushrooms and in summer, wild berries.

The greenhouse is where we butcher meat and take

off our boots and wash our clothes and take our showers and baths. Every cloudless day the sun blasting through the panes warms the rock floor. In turn the floor holds this heat and gives it back slowly at night. Cleaning this floor is as easy as turning over a bucket of water. Spilled potting soil, muddy bootprints, and elk blood wash off the flat stepping stones and down through three inches of gravel and down through two feet of cobblestones to the dirt below.

The week before Thanksgiving we moved in. Already winter had hold of the land. I've seen beautiful snowstorms and dull snowstorms. This one was ugly. Through a foot of snow we stumbled back and forth, cold to the bone, the wind first behind us hurrying us along, then in front of us strafing our cheeks with sleet. We emptied the trailer. We emptied the tent. We filled up the rooms of our home.

What luxury! There was so much space and warmth and light. During the stormy days that followed I did nothing but walk through each room, working out three years' worth of kinks. During the little let-ups in the storm Stew and the boys emptied the storage shed and filled up the loft with boxes of things. There were boxes labeled JAN'S GIFTS and boxes labeled IN CASE OF FIRE DO NOT SAVE. These boxes were shoved unopened into a far corner of the loft. The boxes labeled WINTER CLOTHES and the boxes labeled TOYS were opened with a mixture of curiosity and pleasure, everything inside having been packed so many years ago. "Hey, do you remember this?" we called to each other. The boxes labeled LIVING ROOM, KITCHEN, BEDROOM, and BATH were opened in a froth of excitement, like Christmas presents. In these boxes were the house-warming gifts my mother had sent over the years so our home would lack nothing of the niceties. So many presents, we cook with them, we eat off them, we sleep under them.

Living room and eat-in kitchen.

Boxes were unpacked and things were set in the corners of the rooms until Stew found time to make shelves, closets, and tables to hold them. I moved a few things around to satisfy my sense of order. Moved a few more.

What was supposed to be the master bedroom became a workshop that winter filled with saws and sawhorses and sawdust. Here Stew worked his magic, turned the sorriest pieces of scrap lumber and log ends into tables, chairs, desks, and beds, furniture as beautiful and simple and functional as our home.

Somewhere mixed in with the history of this first winter is the birth of my vocation, my rather unremarkable vocation, as a freelance writer and photographer, a vocation, by the way, I take as seriously as my circumstances permit—as in no telephone, no fax machine, no computer. Here I am living in the most beautiful place in the world and all I can think about is how to get a computer. Stew wants a computer, too. He sees it as a means of cracking open the Forest Service's top-secret files.

In any case, that February, using my old reliable Royal, I wrote the story about how we built our home. After rewriting it six times, having declared myself written out, I sent it off with lots of pictures to the *Mother Earth News*. My reasons for writing were honorable. This wasn't for money, for profit. I wanted to teach people, to inspire them, to purge their very souls. I wanted to alter the course of human events. Also I wanted to get through February.

The next few weeks dragged themselves unwilling along. Time crept by at its most contrary pace as I awaited word from *Mother*. And then it came, the envelope holding my future. Yes they wanted to publish my story and my pictures. Yes, yes, and yes again! Their response, enclosed with a check for five hundred dollars, marked the happiest day of my life. The second happiest day of my life came months later. There in the mailbox was *Mother*, handsome Stew in Kodachrome spread clear across the cover.

Well what budding writer wouldn't be inspired with such a smashing success. I began pitching queries to all the magazines concerned with country living. How about a thousand-word piece on building log caches? on foraging for wild foods? on backpacking? on hunting? on gardening? Dear *Mother*: This is the twelfth story I am submitting for your consideration.

My ideas did not sweep editors off their feet. My typed inspirations came back at me like bounced checks, with impersonal rejection slips attached. My queries still come back at me. Lovely money does not roll in. Nobody in town comes up to me and says they read my story and loved it. Too many of my stories go unread, too many of my pictures appear nowhere. Nevertheless I remain undaunted. This is not a case of publish or perish. I need only enough money to keep me in typing paper, ribbons, film, and lenses. If it was just the money I wouldn't write.

What a thrill it is to reach people through stories. I am always overwhelmed and delighted when readers respond to what I do manage to get published. Over the years their letters, some of them pages long, have somehow found their way to our mailbox.

From Hensel, ND: You are living out the dream I have always had.

From College Station, TX: I was impressed with your decision to make your dramatic break from the hectic doldrums of city life. So often I wish I had the courage to do likewise.

From Mobile, AL: When I lay in bed at night, listening to the police and ambulance sirens, I long for the peace you have found.

From Arcadia, FL: After reading your account, my wife and I decided to dump the rat race and sell our home. We bought a place in northern Idaho and soon will begin our exodus to a simpler life.

There were so many letters. We ignored those from the crazies lest they become encouraged. To those that began, "I've got tons of questions for you," we sent warm helpful replies. Then in the winter of 1993, *Harrowsmith Country Life* published one of my stories, and in the following issue, this reader's response:

The vista portrayed in the Churchwells' photograph of Idaho's Van Horn Peak would look a lot better if they had not built their eyesore of a cabin in the middle of it. "The Cabin on Sawmill Creek" is a sad commentary on people's penchant for owning a piece of paradise and destroying it in the process.

It is also a testament to the Churchwells' hypocrisy
and that of those like them whose environmental
consciousness begins on the other side of their
newly erected fences.

More than once I read this letter to Stew, my voice
more than a bit whimpery. I would have given anything to
see his face liven at some point in my recital, express some
trace of emotion, of anger, of outrage. At the eyesore part
and the hypocrisy part, Stew would always raise his hand
to silence my little pained outcries. Over and over I read
this letter until, by infinite increments, it became less
threatening to me. When I finally finished stomping
around the room, shaking the magazine at Stew, a strange
idea came into my head. I reacted as a writer. Hey, I can
use this in my book.

Having lived in the cabin on Sawmill Creek for over
ten years now we have reached some conclusions. Had we
to build it again, and indeed we would build it again, not
that we would want to build it again, mind you, just thinking about all that work makes me want to lie down and
never get up. But next time we would build the greenhouse bigger, lots bigger. Other than that there would be
no other changes, mistakes being quite insignificant, and
surprisingly few, considering Stew's motley crew.

I wish I could write that this crew stayed together,
lived happily ever after in the cabin on Sawmill Creek or
if not ever after then at least until the boys had fully
grown. But even here in Family Paradise, life is imperfect.
There is nothing permanent but change itself. Nothing
stays the same no matter how much we want it to. So
there you are. The boys are gone. Only Stew and I are here
to build the memories. We are settled here, or as settled as

we ever hope to be. And what's good here just keeps getting a little bit better.

Today, Roy, over six feet tall all of a sudden and with a beard like Eric the Red, having completed two years at the College of Southern Idaho, is attending the University of Idaho, majoring in biology as you might have guessed. In summer he works for the Challis National Forest, counting salmon in the creeks, tracking wolves in the forests, watching raptors on their nests (he actually gets paid for this). Although he loved living on Sawmill Creek, being the oldest of the brothers he was the first to leave, the first to begin life in public high school. When he was a sophomore he found a family in Challis who would board him. Then he enrolled himself in Challis High where he earned enough scholarships for college. He writes home often. He drives up and skis up to see us, gives each of us a little spasm of a hug and lays on my cheek a scratchy kiss. He talks to us about our life, his life, and just life in general. Roy is a good boy, a good son, the best of sons. And Chad isn't so very far from that.

Unlike Roy, even as a preadolescent, Chad never liked living on Sawmill Creek. I don't mean his early years were miserable or even consciously unhappy. But he was, no doubt, dissatisfied. While he was with us, he was not of us. He never found anything to relate to here. He was so lonesome. He longed for the company of other kids, kids he could talk to, kids who would listen to him, follow him around, like him. Roy was too serious all the time, too much in his own world, too into nature.

When Chad's hormones started rioting he went beyond lonely. He began truly hating it here, hating the cramped social sphere, hating his forced isolation from a world he loved, the very same world his parents thought had gone rotten. He developed an attitude. My parents, man. They're so impossibly old and out of touch. They're so demanding.

One winter Chad revolted against his chores, against his schoolwork, against everything he could think of. He would stomp into the refuge of his bedroom because of something I said or something Stew said or something we hadn't said. Then this kid who was always talking just stopped talking. We were afraid he would run away from home, slogging through the snow, hitch-hiking along the highway, taking rides from homicidal crazies, unable to imagine that one bad thing could ever happen to him. And where would he go? Where?

Stew and I decided that, like Roy, Chad needed to brave his way through Challis High. So we went from one unsympathetic friend to another more unsympathetic still, looking for someone who would board him. No luck. Then we dumped the problem on the school board, told them to send up a bus, at which point they declared all of Morgan Creek Road a "no transportation zone," meaning it was too dangerous for a bus route. Fresh out of ideas we laid the problem at the door of Grandma Churchwell, who had been waiting through all this with wings stretched wide to enfold her grandson, her baby. Some baby! Chad was fifteen when we turned him loose on the small-town society of Bird City, Kansas. He has never returned to Sawmill Creek, not even for a visit.

Chad, now grown up, or at any rate grown larger, is now a jock at some agricultural school in Kansas. I can't comment much further than that, he writes home so little, barely once a year. Most of our news comes from Stew's mother and from Roy who Chad telephones regularly in costly installments. Through the years we have seen clippings from the *Bird City Times*, pictures of Chad posing with the Christian youth group, the Future Farmers of America, the scouts, Chad in basketball shorts, in football jerseys, in wrestling sweats, his brown hair cropped short, his jaw squared off at the chin, his blue eyes atwinkle, cocky as always, happy at last.

The boys' absence makes more of a statement than their chattering presence ever did. Nevertheless, Stew and I have adjusted. You see, we have this dog Cujo who gives us just about everything the boys once gave us: companionship, confusion, aggravation, wet sloppy kisses.

The cabin has adjusted too. The bedroom we named for Chad is now Stew's office where he carries on his campaign to save central Idaho from ruin. The room originally planned as the master bedroom (which became Stew's workshop, then the boys' schoolroom) is now my office in fall where I write stories about central Idaho, hoping to spark some interest in protecting the wonders here. In our not so very different ways Stew and I aim to keep this country unspoiled, not only for our future, but for the boys' futures as well, should they ever decide to come home.

4
The Garden

Once I went so far as to slaughter a woodchuck
which ravaged my bean-field . . . and devour him,
partly for experiment's sake.
    –Henry David Thoreau

Having survived our first winter in the cabin on Sawmill Creek, we were around to witness the springtime awakening, the changes that came daily to this vast white silence. As the days lengthened the snow melted and grasses began to grow, grew even as I watched. Wildflowers grew to relieve the greenness of the view. Flocks of migrants flew in and the forests were thick with birds, birds chasing, birds nesting, birds resting, birds bathing in the creek, birds bathing in the rain, birds singing, birds out-singing the general chorus, no longer taking turns, their urges grown more urgent as spring rushed on. I spend vast amounts of time with birds (albeit with brief sojourns among flowers and butterflies). I don't so much worship birds as contemplate them, hour after hour, day after day. I don't so much witness spring as soar through it.

Unlike me, Stew tends to ignore spring, especially when there's work to be done. And there was lots of work to be done even though the house was almost finished (it has been almost finished for years).

After that first winter Stew turned our mighty efforts to landscaping the yard, not with ornamentals but with plants we could eat, plants that would contribute variety and vitamins to our monotonous menus of beans and wild meat.

Being volcanic in nature, Sawmill Canyon is rich in topsoil. Our garden site would have been rich in topsoil had it not been bulldozed over the hillside with the native grasses, wildflowers, and rose bushes. Then while building the house we drove the pickup across the yard, repeatedly, unavoidably, thereby compacting the raw clay. Before we could grow as much as a measly turnip, the ground had to be replaced.

Stew gave the boys a shovel, a pick, and a wheelbarrow. He pointed them to the garden site marked off with sticks and strings–a long narrow rectangle on the south side of the house, extending the entire length of the house (over the years we have doubled the length of the garden, a plot at a time). The boys dug until the long brown rectangle of clay was dug away a foot deep. With the clay they patched potholes in the driveway.

Meanwhile Stew drove the pickup down the driveway to the creek where I was waiting with two more shovels. An hour or so later he drove the pickup back up the driveway, the bed filled with topsoil, rich topsoil, none richer. After filling in the entire rectangle, it took dozens of trips, I raked it smooth and subdivided it into plots, each three feet across, several yards long, and separated by walkways wide enough to work in. And there you have it, our garden, over a dozen plots mounded with topsoil, squirming with earthworms.

Stew and I have collaborated on a few projects like this, but on most, there has been a suspect division of labor. You see, Stew is capable where I lack the knack, all my training having to do with counting money. Also there is something about my genes. I can't hammer a nail in straight no matter how many private hours of patient instruction I am given. I can only get a sense of how things like water rams work, the details being hopelessly beyond me. Not that I'm moronic mind you, but there's something about heavy thinking that confuses me, drives me nuts.

So Stew has assigned us roles in this back-to-the-land adventure, meaning, he gets to be construction foreman, master mechanic, great white hunter, and I get to be his stooge. He gets to be cook, or I should say, *Chef de Cuisine*, and I get to be the dish washing drudge. This is because he is a connoisseur of fine foods; tasting is an intense experience for him not far removed from real ecstasy. And me? I like to eat, with both fists, the kind of food served at truck stops.

I get to be the gardener, too, because . . . well . . . I forget just why, I wonder why, I was neither a good gardener nor an experienced gardener, rather not a gardener at all. Perhaps it had to do with the potted begonias I somehow managed to keep alive on the windowsill of my condo. More likely it was because Stew just didn't want to be the gardener, all that hoeing and weeding and watering, all that frustration and failure, and for what, for a harvest about as bountiful as you might expect in a climate too high, too dry, too cold for the cultivation of crops.

Before moving to Sawmill Canyon I didn't know beans about growing beans, or growing greens, or growing anything else besides begonias. Some of what I know about gardening I know from books like *Gardening Without Work* by Ruth Stout and from magazines like *Mother Earth News* and *Harrowsmith Country Life*. Some of what I know about gardening I know from fellow gardeners in Challis (I would pick through their brains as readily as I would pick through their plots). But most of what I know, the most reliable part of what I know, I know from my own downhearted experiences.

Horticulture is not part of my heritage. My childhood memories hold scenes of Palm Springs as it was in the good old days, the days before irrigation projects and sprayed chemicals turned this land of cactus and sand into a land of lawns, fairways, and country club estates. I remember one year my mother planted a huge plot of lettuce in our backyard, just lettuce, as an experiment. First the jackrabbits had their share. Then the grasshoppers had the rest. Forevermore she harvested vegetables from grocery bins at the market, which is something I should seriously consider.

There are only two seasons in Palm Springs – summer and not summer. There are only three seasons in Challis – July, August, and winter – or so people like to tell newcomers from Palm Springs (along with another line that goes something like, "If you don't like this weather, stick around, it will change in an hour"). In spite of their short growing season, Challis gardeners harvest squash and corn and tomatoes and melons and apples and . . . well, the list is long, their harvest is big, so big they brag about it as if it were a medal of honor.

On Sawmill Creek, about a thousand feet higher than Challis, the growing season is shorter by sixty days. In other words, my growing season is only a month long, on the best of years. All that is predictable about the weather here is that it can't be predicted accurately. You can get a bad sunburn on the tenth of June and be wading through inches of fresh snow on the twenty-fifth. It snows in July or it rains steadily for weeks or it never rains enough or long enough to be useful. Come August, the rain clouds never make it over Van Horn Peak but the cold fronts do and when they do my potato plants freeze and die, the spuds still smaller than golf balls.

If it's not the weather, then it's the unruly gangs of deer, and if not the deer, then the porcupines or the gophers or the ground squirrels or the snowshoe hares or the voles or the grasshoppers or the cabbage worms or the flea beetles or some combination of the above or all of the above. Of course, these challenges I face would be best met by bowing to nature's will, to nature's authority, by knuckling under if it comes to that, and often it comes to that. I firmly believe this. But my desire, my so very human desire to conquer nature, to have my way with nature, is a desire of the highest order. What it has come to on Sawmill Creek is not so much a war of wills but an uneasy truce.

Snowshoe hare

Anyway, as I was saying, Stew laid it all on me, the varmints, the weather, the work, and it all begins with the coming of seed catalogs, in February, when the snow covering the garden is higher than my thighs and green growing things are mere fantasies. I sit beside the stove, thumbing though a dozen seed catalogs, sighing, passing pages of pumpkins grand as coaches and corn high as an elephant's eye. I can't grow pumpkins the size of peas or corn even squat or tomatoes without a greenhouse or melons without miracles or apples or beans or broccoli or brussel sprouts or . . . well, the list is long, my harvest is small, so small I don't even like to talk about it.

After the seed packets arrive I fill my journal with sketches of plots that rotate year after year with plants that thrive on adversity: lettuce, peas, root vegetables, cole crops, a few culinary herbs. That's all. Nothing else. Out of these plants I'll be lucky to get one-two-three good crops.

I used to experiment and still do to some extent. One year I wondered if sunflowers would grow. I wanted to cut down on my bird-feeding bill. In June I planted a dozen seeds and in August I was surprised and more than a little thrilled to see them blooming brazenly above the potato plants. Then a cold front cleared Van Horn Peak and froze their flowery heads and undeveloped seeds. The Jerusalem artichokes I also tried also thrived but produced tubers too stunted to make harvesting worthwhile, all that digging for just a few bites of something that wasn't all that delicious.

The fruit bushes I planted seven years ago are thriving. They might even bear cherries and elderberries if only I could figure out how to keep the deer from deflowering their branches every spring and pruning the stems to stubble. They don't really prune, those deer, they ruin, they desecrate, they so discouraged the asparagus from growing it came back less vigorously every year and one year it came back not at all. Now the old asparagus bed and the artichoke bed and the sunflower bed grow thick stalks of ruby red rhubarb. What else might grow as well as rhubarb? I'm still experimenting, maybe Chinese celery, maybe fava beans, maybe this, maybe that. Gardening you learn every year. You don't get it all at once.

March 15: The low last night was five degrees, the high today thirty-five. It was breezy, blue, beautiful with five inches of new snow on the ground. I worked in the greenhouse most of the day, filling flats with potting soil, then with seeds—tomatoes, peppers, onions, cabbages, beets, nasturtiums, dill.

The greenhouse is heated only by the sun. The temperature in there drops below freezing after sunset. So until May, Stew and I have to lug all these flats indoors to the mantle above the stove where they spend the night. Until July, nights in the greenhouse are still colder than pepper plants and tomato plants like, so we have to shuttle them into the bathroom where they spend the nights crowded together on the platform Stew built for the bathtub (at least this space has not been wasted). This is not what you would call easy on the back, shuttling twenty jumbo pots of tall stems and vines towering over their stakes. Why we even grow peppers and tomatoes in our climate has everything to do with the salsa Stew makes for venison tortillas. You see, Stew cut his teeth on hot spicy food. He craves it, can't live without it, the hotter the better. Myself, I crave sweets, and it goes beyond my comprehension why some people savor not so much the flavor of spicy food but the fierceness, the flame, the pain.

April Fools' Day: The low last night was twenty-five degrees, the high today forty-two. It was sunny, warm, wonderful working in the garden. I forked frozen mulch off the plots so the sun will defrost the soil, that is, if the weather holds, if the weather holds.

Ah, spring. When will I ever learn it is not a changed event but a perpetually changing event. Every year I am fooled by the weather and astounded by my foolishness. Every May, whenever it's unseasonably sunny and Sawmill Canyon is beginning to bloom and the birds are all singing their love songs, I cannot control my urge to get out and garden even though it's weeks too early to garden and if I just wanted to get out of the house I could get out and hike or smell the flowers or follow birds around. I can't explain it to myself, this urge, any more than I can explain it to anyone else. Even if I could explain it who would understand, nobody but other nuts who find joy in working with dirt, getting it under their nails, splitting their nails, gnarling their knuckles, getting their palms calloused, rough as an old boot, getting their backs all bent out of whack.

At any rate here I am shoveling dirt weeks too early, turning over the plots when they are wet (which explains the big dirt clods I can never get rid of). Here I am shoveling earthworms, bringing them squirming to the surface (which explains the yard full of robins making the most of their opportunities).

There are people who find great joy in watching the seeds they have planted push their way through the dirt, stitch their way across the plots like so many little green inches. I am one of those people. That's why on some years, during a succession of summery days, I seed my plots too early, knowing from experience it's too early even for cold-hardy plants, knowing from experience that the following weeks of more typical spring weather, of hard freezes and snowstorms and strings of sunless days, will bring flea beetles into my plots (which explains the tiny holes in my little green inches). Needless to say even if my seedlings manage to survive the beetles and the weather they never grow enough to notice.

May Day: The low last night was eighteen degrees, the high today twenty-nine. Snow squalls, sleet, slush. Around midmorning Stew took up his rifle, reluctantly took up his rifle, his .22, and shot dead two woodpeckers, the same two flickers that have been hammering on the gable ends of the house, stopping just short of the tar paper. What Stew kills we eat. It's a new rule around here. Call it Churchwell's First Law. Like it or not, flickers are for dinner.

I went into the garden and found multiplying onions multiplying, growing green above the slush. With an artful chopping of his knive, Stew cut them into bits and stirred them into a brown gravy, a gravy that was supposed to make the flickers go down easier. Well I chewed and chewed and chewed and still I gagged. I suppose there's some kind of justice in that.

The first warm week in June, I plant seeds for a second time. And I plant potatoes. And I transplant the greenhouse seedlings. Throughout the summer as the plants reach for the sun I tuck mulch around their stems and blanket their beds. Mulch modifies temperature extremes, somewhat, and smothers weeds, sort of, or so the gardeners in Challis keep telling me.

Rain-rotten hay is my mulch of choice. The ranchers haul it in bales to the Custer County landfill and Stew and I haul it home, or we used to anyway. We used to haul home bundles of old newspapers, too, for starting the stoves, and all kinds of useful things, things Stew says he's going to fix someday, like that pitchfork with the broken handle, that barbecue with the broken wheel. Like traditional scroungers everywhere, whenever we made a run to the dump we came home with more than we took in.

We were so disappointed to see the dump change. These changes were hard to miss, hard to ignore. There was a new chain-link fence. There was a guard stationed at the gate. There were all those signs everywhere: NO SCAVENGING. They weren't kidding either.

Why these changes came about had something to do

with broken glass, an injury, a lawsuit. Nevertheless, for those of us hooked on mulch, not to mention recycling, lawlessness was justifiable. When the guard wasn't looking Stew and I continued to heave hay bales into the back of the pickup. (Oh, grab that old hoe. Sure it's broken but I'll fix it). The camper shell concealed our theft but not our shit-eating grins.

A few years ago the dump changed again. The commissioners of Custer County, always tight with the taxpayers' bucks, decided to get out of the dumping business entirely. It was too darn expensive to keep running the dump, what with new water quality laws taking effect. So now our household trash goes into a row of Dempsey Dumpsters guarded by a mean old man with eyes like an eagle. From there it goes to the Lemhi County landfill over sixty miles away. Nowadays if you want to dump anything the guard doesn't consider household trash you have to pay him a fee. He will then point you to any number of sites where you can dump your scraps of lumber, your pruned tree limbs, your broken hoes, your dead pigs. Because of this fee people now keep everything they used to throw away, including, should you be wondering, spoiled hay.

It goes beyond the scope of this book to describe why filched hay works better than store-bought hay. And really, do you care? Fortunately my earthworms don't. They grind up whatever I feed them. In turn they make food my plants can use. As a result I don't need chemical fertilizers. I don't need a tiller either. As the worms burrow through my plots they aerate the soil and drain it when it rains too hard.

Mulch keeps the plots moist between rain and snow showers but never enough to forgo irrigation. In the years gone by, thankfully gone by, when I was left to my own primitive devices, irrigation was a time-diddling, day-

wasting chore. Like Mary Mary of storybook fame I provided each plant with a personal shower out of a watering
can. Even then I considered myself lucky. I could fill the
can at the faucet; I didn't have to haul water from the
creek. Then I got even luckier. My Sugarbear built me a
tank into the hillside above the house. Now I irrigate with
garden hoses, just like everybody else. I even have one of
those magic wands, the kind with five spray patterns from
dribble to flash flood.

I've got it made. Or I've almost got it made. In order to
reach the beets at the far end of the yard I have to yank
the kinks out of six garden hoses hooked end-to-end-to-
end-to-end-to . . . Then I have to thread my way down the
aisles, going slowly and carefully, lest the hoses catch the
corners of the plots and uproot the crops. While I am working my way down the aisles I notice things, like how the
onions are in bad need of weeding, how the snowshoe
hares have been at the lettuce again, how the humming-
birds are feeding on the pale pink flowers that will devel-
op, hares permitting, into peas. As I pass the jungle of pea
vines, a rufous hummingbird zips up, materializes inches
from my nose, and with wings whirring, probes the red
visor shading my face. He perches on the pea fence, clasp-
ing the top strand of wire, his feet tiny as tendrils, curled
like tendrils. He flashes throat feathers metallic orange.
Ooh! Wow!

After watering the beets I water the potatoes. All
around me, off to my left, off to my right, tree swallows
with their iridescent green feathers and barn swallows
with their orange and blue feathers swoop and soar on a
level with my eyes, appearing, disappearing, now I see
them, now I don't. The minutes go by. The water puddles
in the aisles. The barn swallows notice the mud I have
unwittingly made. They scoop it up for their nest, a nest
they are determined to make under the west end of the

roof, despite my arm-waving protests. As I do every year I'll have to scrub off the porch deck, the willow chairs, the end tables, the gooey mess their nestlings make.

Under an awning of potato leaves a house wren finds shelter from my shower. The wren (he's actually more feathered mouse than bird) grabs an insect, a bad bug I hope, a potato beetle or a potato moth or a potato worm. Beak firmly clamped around whatever he caught, the wren flies to the nesting box nailed to the corner fence post. Into the hole goes the wren. Out the hole comes insect-like chanting. Out the hole comes the wren. To the top of the woodpile go both wrens, dancing with agitation. "Watch out. Watch out. Over there. Over there." I see it too, a weasel prowling among the logs, looking for wrenlets and other assorted youngsters.

While I water the carrots I watch mixed flocks of juncos, redpolls, siskins, finches, sparrows, and doves, all feeding wing-to-wing beside the garden where the unplanted clay of the parking lot has been colonized by some kind of creeping plant rich in seeds, some kind of weed that weaves itself into everything I plant. Under the watchful eyes of the Cooper's hawk these birds feed and scratch and peck and fight over seed rights, these birds, I call them "my" birds, knowing full well I don't own them any more than I own the sun and moon.

Suddenly the yard explodes. In a collective spasm of fear the flocks fly up, disappear into thin air, every last bird, gone. The Cooper's hawk lands on the bird feeder and with wild hungry eyes glares at the grasses hiding his prey. I give my heart to the tiny siskin *and* the Cooper's hawk that snatches it away.

In 1898, nature writer Neltje Blanchan wrote that the Cooper's hawk "lives by devouring birds of so much greater value than itself that the law of survival of the fittest should be enforced by lead until these villains, from being the commonest of their generally useful tribe, adorn museum cases only." When I read this it disturbed me. It disturbs me still. This dividing all wildlife into "good and bad" exists today, this attitude rooted more deeply than dandelions. It more than exists, it thrives throughout certain central Idaho communities. Also in these communities there exists that ages-old system of avian classification that lumps together golden eagles and hawks (all hawks, be they red-tailed hawks, sharp-shinned hawks, rough-legged hawks, Cooper's hawks) into what is known hereabouts as a "chicken hawk." Of course, all eagles and hawks are protected by law. But in these communities, where neighbors live miles apart, gunshots are seldom heard. Like when nobody's looking, the airspace above certain ranches, the birds in that airspace, belong to the ranchers.

For those of us not into raising chickens, watching a Cooper's hawk capture a bird in midair is thrilling. Watching him capture a cabbage-fat vole is more than thrilling, it's joyous. Yet I must admit, and it is with shame I do so, there was a time not long ago I felt differently. You see, the damn hawk ate my bluebird.

Sometimes you just know that such-and-such is so although you can't prove it in any physical way. I simply took it on faith that this bluebird was the same bluebird that had perched on the ridgepole as soon as it was in place. For five springs he perched under the roof of the porch, waiting out storms. For five summers he perched on the pitchfork (I stuck it in a bale of hay so he would perch where I could see him better). I would raise my eyes from the rows, my hands on the hoe, and just stand there, so bewitched was I by his incredible blueness. Like others before me I tried to describe this blueness, tried to match it with forget-me-nots, with autumn skies, with Stew's eyes.

For five summers this bluebird took turns with his paler partner guarding the nesting box on the fence two posts over from the wrens. While he was perched there the Cooper's hawk got him, struck him down, dead. I found his feathers below the box, a pathetic pile of them, all just feathers now, so dull in death. I felt such a loss, as did his partner. She had to finish raising their brood by herself.

Next spring a new bluebird came, the one I have now. He also perches on the ridgepole, under the porch, on the pitchfork, on the nesting box. He was born in that box, I know it, he was part of that brood, he's that blue. Actually, he's more than *that* blue, he's really, really blue.

What is it about these birds that so distracts me I forget to water some plots entirely and water other plots so sopping wet the earthworms surface gasping for air. Sometimes I even water the aisles. No wonder weeds have taken hold. Nature abhors bare dirt. One day these weeds, these impudent, importunate weeds, these Perennials From Hell, will take over the whole garden, the whole yard. They will claim what was once theirs, what by all rights should still be theirs. These weeds are waiting, seeking not sunlight, or fertilizer, or water, or space. Just time. Patiently, eternally, they wait for us to go back the way we came.

I have drawn a line around my garden where weeds cannot cross or they will be slaughtered, not chemically of course, never chemically, but mechanically, with a shovel, a weed whip, a hoe. I dig up the wild roses when they cross the line in pursuit of the peas. I slash back the waves of foxtail barley whose seeds came sneaking in, hidden in bales of hay. I hack back the prickly lettuce and wild buckwheat that came from Europe generations ago and the dandelions that came from next door. The dandelions flourish next door, on cow pies. They send their cottony bolls afloating on wind-given paths, afloating over the

fence, afloating into my irrigated plots where they go readily, speedily to seed.

There are turnip seedlings growing in the onion patch,
sown there last fall by the wind. There are potato
seedlings growing in the cabbage patch, sprouted from the
spuds I missed during the harvest last fall. The volunteer
peas don't care where they grow, but I do, I want them in
the pea patch, I want only cabbages in the cabbage patch.
These peas are no better than weeds. I yank them up by
their roots.

The clover has to go. I yank it up, hoe it up, dig it up,
and still it thrives. I don't so much stop the clover from
spreading as I make it spread faster, like crabgrass. See,
one year I let just this one little clover plant take hold in
the pea plot, thinking how a little clover would be good, it
would be a living mulch, it would feed my friends the bees
and distract the snowshoe hares. Well this was a little
something I should have looked into first. Faster than I
would have thought possible, the clover took over the pea
plot, the aisles on both sides, the next plots, all the plots,
all the aisles, everywhere, I'll never get rid of it. It's scary.
I have not yet worked out what to do. But that's a problem
for another day.

Something else I haven't worked out is what to do
about the weeds of the animal kingdom, when out of the
forest and into my oasis of exotic greenery they come
sneaking, snaking, burrowing, waddling, hopping, buzzing,
floating, crawling on four legs, crawling on six legs, crawling on many legs. Of course, not all wild creatures are bad
for gardens. This is a truism worn thin by repetition, but
it's still true. Consider ladybugs and lacewings, the pit-
bulls of beneficial insects, and centipedes, predatory
wasps, warblers, wrens, garter snakes, shrews, these I welcome heartily. The rest are like clover. There isn't much I
can do about them short of poisoning my oasis.

Above the lettuce and cabbage plots pretty white butterflies float in fleets. I am not concerned. When I harvest
the heads I simply pluck off their green wormy offspring. I
have found that a broad-minded attitude deals best with
the worms I have overlooked, the lively worms Stew so
carelessly tosses in our dinner salads. "So spit 'em out!"
Stew isn't one to mince words as I am not one to mince
worms.

Worms have never wrecked a crop (or a dinner guest
for that matter). But I can't say the same about voles,
those rodents loved by nobody, those mouse look-alikes
that tunnel under my garden, leaving my plots looking
like sponge cake. Ever wonder why children's stories fea-
ture cute little mice, even moles, but never voles? Well I
don't. What they do isn't cute. They chew cabbage heads
beyond recognition and potato plants beyond recovery.
This is not a pretty sight. I swear I can hear them right
now, calling back and forth to each other. "Are you eating
the peas yet? We're eating the peas, are you? Spuds are
ready. Pass it on."

My trouble with voles comes in cycles, every three or
four years, when their populations explode. Voles are ordi-
nary, in no way mysterious or romantic like their kissing
cousins the famous lemmings you see in wildlife films,
migrating en masse, swarming through forests and towns
and cities, crossing rivers and ridges and all other barriers
in their frenzied drive to find food. Since the sea is just
another barrier to be crossed, the lemmings, thousands
and thousands of them, dive in, swim to exhaustion, and
drown en masse.

Without a sea anywhere near, or even a lake, it is left
to me and my primitive devices to control these voles when
their populations reach flood stage. Believe me this is way
beyond Havahart traps. This is a take-no-prisoners roden-
ticide I commit, I unwillingly commit. I do it for the sake

of my garden, for the health of the vole community, for the greater good of mankind.

Nowadays I log many vole kills. I should feel sorrier about this than I do. My callousness comes from years of frustration, years of lost crops and failed schemes.

In the beginning I tried trapping the voles with mousetraps, for what are voles but simply mud-colored mice. I bought a dozen traps, baited them with butter, and had Stew set the springs on the traps because my hands shake with nervousness when setting traps and I keep snapping my fingers. Silently the voles watched from their hidey-holes as Stew laid the traps around the garden. Next morning the traps were gone, every last one, never to be found.

The dreaded Monster of Sawmill Canyon.

So there I was buying a dozen more traps, staking them to the ground so they wouldn't disappear. Stew baited them first with butter, then with peanut butter, then with cheese, nothing worked all that well. Most of the voles were just too tricky to trap, and the few blockheads I did manage to brain didn't make a dent in the ever-expanding population, the numbers behind the numbers.

I cursed the voles mightily, not for the first time, not for the last. Suddenly out of my frustration came a burst of light and I leaped excitedly to my feet. I would create a flash flood. I would send a wall of water raging through their subterranean runways. I would drown these voles in their bed chambers, in their nurseries, in their granaries, as they ate, as they mated, as they slept. I started the ram pump. I turned my magical wand to "flash flood." I stuck it down a hole. Five minutes passed. Nothing. Eight minutes passed. Still nothing. Twelve minutes. The pump went thump-thump-thump, beat for beat with my heart. I got tired of standing. I sat down. Sixteen minutes. Just as I was running out of patience, there! and there! and there! out came the voles, out their back doors and front doors and side doors, voles running, sputtering, on the verge of mass hysteria, heading en masse for the meadow. At some point—I wasn't there but some things you just know—they groomed themselves dry, returned to their voley lives, and did some more begetting. One little, two little, three little voles . . . four little, five little . . . and more on the way.

I firmly believe when a person is faced with a desperate situation, violence, if it is sincere and pure of heart, is justifiable. I hated these voles, sincerely, purely of heart, with a rancid hatred that was becoming unhealthy. I am not proud of what I did next (and perhaps I'm telling too much here).

One day, shovel in hand, with voley eyes on me, all sixty pairs, all the time, I was patching my garden plots, filling the vole holes, when I just went berserk, bonkers. I yanked up my cabbages, my peas, my potatoes, by their roots, trying to gain access to the voles' underground chambers. Once I got hold of the shovel, there was no stopping me. Mulch flying, dirt flying, earthworms flying, I dug up my turnips, carrots, and beets, left them for dead. In disgust and delight, I dug up nests and voles, pregnant mamas and their wee trembling babes, stomped them all with my brutal boots. I looked around at the carnage, innocently, as if it had nothing to do with me. Oh my, oh my, oh my. It was so horrible. It was more than horrible. All my plants were dead but hardly any voles.

Stew has these big shoulders I can cry on. I sought relief in his dependable wisdom although at times I get this feeling he considers my dependence on his wisdom a form of weakness I should try to overcome. This was one of those times. He listened to the steady yapping of my voice, showed enthusiasm for every detail, pretended high interest, then told me he couldn't help me, right then anyway. He couldn't just pull a solution out of his hat. It would take time, and he didn't have the time. What the wretches were doing to my vegetables, the vegetables he also liked to eat, was a matter of little concern to him. This was my problem, exclusively, a gardener's problem, and if I was going to be the gardener, I should solve it myself. I didn't think to ask him, if I wasn't going to be the gardener, then who was?

That a solution was eventually found was of course inevitable, or I wouldn't have had a garden to write about. As it turned out, Roy, my budding biologist, was the hero of the day.

Roy had read in his biology textbook all about voles, how they are related to lemmings. More important, he had read about a kind of rodent trap scientists use in the field. Ever the clever kid, he made one of these traps, or something similar anyway, by cutting the tops off plastic gallon-size jugs, the kind of jugs syrup and vinegar come in. He planted these jugs in the ground wherever the voles exited their burrows. Then he filled them with water three inches deep.

That night and for many nights thereafter, when the voles and their progeny and their grand-progeny went swarming through the forest of vegetables, or what was left of the vegetables, they tried to cross these watery barriers in their frenzied drive to find more vegetables. They dove into the traps, swam to exhaustion, and drowned en masse. I love it! I love it! But I hate myself for loving it.

Even so, there are some years when I think gardening in this wilderness is an impossible dream, an impractical endeavor to which I am nonetheless fanatically devoted (I didn't intend to get devoted to gardening, it just sucked me in). So let's see. What else is there to worry about besides voles? Oh yes. Porcupines. Not so picky, these porcupines. They even savor the hot leaves of my horseradish. If I let porcupines get ahead of me I will not have even a hint of a garden. And not having a garden is way worse than having one.

Unlike voles, porcupines are big and tasty, like a Thanksgiving Day turkey (Stew has this recipe for fricasseed porky I'd die for). Porcupines are easy to kill. When I find signs of them in my garden, pellet-like turds, zigzaggy tail tracks, horseradish plants chewed to the ground, I tell Stew to get his rifle ready. Actually it's our rifle but I don't like to shoot it, like I don't like to set mousetraps, and for basically the same reason.

Porcupines are nocturnal. If I am going to have Stew shoot one, I have to set the alarm clock to buzz me awake in the blurry hours around midnight. The alarm rings. One of us will have to get up. Stew awakens, suddenly, from a poke in the ribs. Hurry up, Stew. No time to waste. Don't put on your pants. Don't put on your shoes. Get the flashlight. Get the rifle.

Clad in his skivvies, barefooted and blinking, Stew gets himself out the door, across the porch, all the way to the garden on the sneak. Then he goes into his porcupine imitation, calling to them in low whimpering moans as they are calling to him. There's movement in the horseradish bed. Out waddles a porcupine and into the beam of the flashlight. BAM! That's it. It's that simple. Stew will spend the next few hours carefully skinning the porcupine, slowly peeling off the needle-sharp hide, the details of which wouldn't hold your interest any more than they hold mine.

What else? Oh yes. The deer. In the nether hours of the night they come bouncing over the fence and tiptoeing, yes tiptoeing, across the yard. They stand there chomping the tops off the beets, just inches from where Cujo the garden-guarder is chained to his doghouse, snoring, sound asleep. Unfortunately (or fortunately, depending upon your point of view) deer are protected in Idaho. If you should be so foolish as to get caught killing a deer out of season, whatever the reason (including self-defense), you will lose face in the community when your crime and your hefty fine appear in the pages of the *Messenger*. When I count up my losses due to deer, when I then consider the only sensible solution, the very thought of Stew disgraced dims my vision of poached venison.

With deer I have also tried everything, every solution known to man, all the home remedies from perfumy soaps to peppery sprays, all the mail-order gimmicks from Scent Fence to Deer-B-Gone. I tried planting more beets on the theory that if you can't beat them, feed them. I tried the firecrackers given to us by the local game cop, the screaming rockets and M-80s he said would scare the deer from hell to breakfast. The result? A loud noise. A big bang. The deer just stood there staring, wagging their ears, then returned to the beet greens at hand, resumed their feeding in earnest, their muzzles buried in our summer salad.

There is nothing, absolutely nothing—there have been studies—that can be done about deer, nothing legal anyway. This is something I often say although it's not quite the case. Years ago, one August, when my crops were most vulnerable, I talked the family into bedding down in the garden for two weeks, just as an experiment.

Stew and I laid our sleeping bags head-to-head on the west end of the garden and the boys laid their sleeping bags head-to-head on the east end. We formed a sort of scent fence that frightened the deer away. But this was such a hassle, having to drag mattresses, sleeping bags, and pillows outside, then shaking off the dirt and dragging them back in. And we never got much sleep, what with the night noises, the hooting owls, the wailing coyotes, the pounding of hooves on the run. However, as I remember, it was not that unpleasant lying there snug in our sacks, sniffing breezes spiced with dill, listening to the beets grow, watching moon rises and stars fall.

One night after weeks of near sleeplessness we slept soundly, too soundly it turned out. Upon awakening we saw how row upon row of Early Wonder beets and Purple Top turnips had been chopped to stumpage, not by deer or porcupines, there were none of the usual signs, but by . . . what?

At first we didn't see it, and then we did, how there were beet greens and turnip tops strewn about, forming almost a pathway to the plywood box that houses the propane bottles. Without a doubt this box also housed the mysterious vandal. I directed Stew to lift the lid. Well someone had to do it. There among the propane bottles, among piles of garden greenery, in the only unvegetated corner of the box, stood this bulky structure of sticks, something that resembled not so much a nest as a mass of debris left behind by floodwaters. But it was a nest, and in this nest stood the nest-maker, (O!) a woodrat. Having never seen such a creature we stared at him as he stared at us and furiously stomped his hind foot. He looked like a huge overfed deer mouse. He was kind of handsome really. Soft brown fur. Big ears. Large eyes. Long whiskers. Squirrel-like tail. He didn't deserve to be called a rat, a name I associate with vermin.

But you couldn't call this woodrat charming, no, I wouldn't use that word. Nevertheless Chad was charmed.

Calling upon his finest theatrics, he gazed adoringly into the propane box and convinced us that he wanted nothing else in the world but to have this creature for a pet. Woody Woodrat. Already he had named him. Already he had decided that this Woody would be a he, not a she. To Chad's way of thinking, a she, especially a pregnant she, meant ratlets, more mouths to feed on Mom's garden.

We read up on Woody. Indeed he was not a rat, not even related to a rat. The habits of woodrats (aka pack-rats) are clean. Their character is playful. In the grandiose opinion of John James Audubon, they make a "far more interesting pet than many others that the caprice of man has from time to time induced him to select."

Let me say in my defense that I am not entirely beyond persuasion. Under my hardness I can be soft. Under my dispassion I can be sentimental. When Chad promised to keep Woody out of my garden I believed him, believed he could, wanted to believe he could, although how he would hadn't been worked out. For reasons not rooted in common sense I agreed to give Woody a chance.

The days went by. My garden grew taller. With any luck, within the week we would be eating lettuce, cabbages, and peas. During this time all I ever saw of Woody was Woody asleep in the propane box and Woody stomping his foot at being so rudely awakened. Now his nest was decorated with shiny things Chad had given him, a ball of tinfoil, a pocket mirror, a dime.

Woody slept all day. He rummaged around all night doing god knows what, borrowing stuff, stealing stuff, decorating his nest with Chad's last dimes. During the hours after dinner, in the evening time of quietness, Woody would perch on the windowsill outside the living room while inside I would try to concentrate on my book, Woody's image coming between me and the words I tried to read. Again and again my eyes would return to my book but it was no use, the words blurred before my eyes.

Perhaps it was the darkness that threw a bad light on Woody, a sinister light. But as I stared out at Woody staring in at me, "handsome" wasn't the word that came to mind. Woody was a rat alright. Round ratty ears. Black beady rat-glittery eyes. Long whiskered snout. He was every bit as repulsive as those rats that hang out in alleys, growning big as ponies on garbage.

More days went by. My garden grew shorter, stumpier. We were not eating lettuce or cabbages or peas or anything else (obviously Chad hadn't worked things out). Suddenly it came to me. Just like that. I saw the purpose to Woody's window-peeping. He wasn't trying to amuse us. He wasn't being curious about us or lonesome for us. What anthropomorphic nonsense! Woody was watching for our bedtime—his harvest time. Not only was he robbing me blind and robbing Chad blind, he was patting himself on his squirrel-like tail about getting away with it. If he kept this up there would be no turnips. No beets. No parsnips. Nothing.

Surely you see where this is all leading. You've noticed how I write of Woody in the past tense. I am not absolutely certain when my long-suffering patience limited out (somewhere between the time I found my new asparagus stalks crammed into the corner of Woody's box and the time we started eating beans). In any case it was me, the gardener, the mean mom, the dreaded monster of the place, who ended it all by putting a contract out on the dirty rat. Stew, always the hit man in this sordid side of business, armed himself with a hoe, the head of which had been straightened out and sharpened with a file. With murder on our minds, Stew and I approached the propane box. I lifted the lid. Woody began stomping his foot and blinking at the unaccustomed daylight, blinking at us, oh, so innocently blinking at us. Stew raised the hoe. He rammed it down, missing most of Woody, just amputating his tail. He raised the hoe again. He rammed it home. Eeeeeuk! Poor Woody was cleft in twain.

Churchwell's First Law: What Stew kills must be eaten, anything bigger than a vole that is. Woody was way bigger than a vole. "End of argument," Stew said. "Now let's see. How about woodrat pate. Or perhaps, skewered rodentine *en brochette*. Yes! Perfect! Now what wine would go best."

Why we didn't eat Woody had more to do with Woody's mangled condition than with the unsettling fact that he had been a kid's cherished pet. In any case Stew had been kidding, had to have been kidding. But Chad didn't think so. This is why, without ceremony, without tears, he rushed to chuck Woody over the hillside. May he rest in peace—I guess. For days thereafter Woody deceased lived on in my cold wicked heart. It was weeks later, long after Woody had turned into grass, that I finally got used to the emptiness at the living room window.

Although I write of Woody in a light-hearted manner, light-hearted was far from what I felt. If there was a light side to any of this, it has been lost in a world of regret. I am not an uncaring person. I want to be an innocent person, a good person. Killing animals makes me feel bad on several levels. Believe me, had I to do it again I would have let Woody live. I would have simply cut my horticultural losses and bought more beans.

You see, when Stew and I came to Sawmill Creek over a decade ago we foolishly expected to coexist peacefully with the wildlife, all forms of wildlife. If you have any romance in your soul you will understand how the abundance and diversity of wildlife brought us here in the first place, keeps us here. Unfortunately like many other caring human beings we tried to manage our land not to suit nature but to suit ourselves, our way of life, and in doing so we brought about change, not all of it bad, mind you, but change nonetheless. Some of this change is too subtle to notice. Some of it, far too much of it, is woefully obvious.

To our credit, whatever that's worth, right from the start we tried to have as little impact as possible. Sometimes we could see beforehand consequences that were unacceptable, like when friends pressed their soft purry kittens on us. There was no discussing it, we wouldn't take them. Sure these kittens would grow into big cats, cats that would kill their weight in voles, daily. But cats would also murder my lovely birds. Nor would we take the fuzzy yellow chicks pressed upon us. The consequences were just as predictable. Coyotes and fox and chicken hawks make good neighbors if they aren't tempted to take easy meals. Eggs aren't essential to our recipes, our good health, or our self-sufficiency.

On the other hand our garden is all of the above and much more. Our garden, in part, keeps us from having to work for wages, for money to buy, well, vegetables, or I should say vegetable stuff, supermarket products raised by strangers, prepared by strangers, pumped full of additives, laced with poisonous residues, tasting like the assembly-line products they are (or meat for that matter, run through a salmonella bath, hacked into convenient parts, and packaged in plastic film). Having to work for wages also means your kids have to wait to hunt and fish, until you have the exact amount of free time. And in the end, does it really make a difference whether you kill in person or by proxy, at the supermarket.

It's a joy to have a garden. It's a greater joy to have wildlife. It's the greatest joy of all to have a garden *and* wildlife. This is what I am working on. If I, serial killer of voles, have failed to find gentler solutions to rodent invasions it isn't for want of trying. I'll find those solutions, if not today, then tomorrow.

In spite of my mighty efforts my garden remains firmly under nature's control, even more firmly now that I have slipped into foolish, tenderhearted, mushy old age (Stew is supposed to step in here and say, "You're not so old"). Well, now that I am oldish, I find I have become quite blind to the chipmunks that force their way through the strawberry netting and steal the luscious red fruit from under my very nose. The strawberries they leave are all the sweeter for being so few.

As I grow older I find I grow fonder of the snowshoe hares than the piddling-few peas they leave. The hares think of me as their friend, their provider. They bring me gifts of their newborns, their crops of perfect miniature babies, who will chew on my shirttail if I hold very still and all but climb into my lap. I have been tempted on occasion to give their heads a little grandmotherly pat.

And the deer? Well when I see the does teach their speckled fawns to leap tall fences my heart sinks and soars at the same time.

The garden feeds my soul in ways beyond measure, in ways, by all rights, it should feed my flesh. Alas, in the end my harvest can be called bountiful by only the imaginative. My beets are small, hardly worth the digging, just what you might expect with their leafy tops chewed to the ground. When I dig potatoes, that is if I have potatoes to dig, meaning their leaves haven't been frozen black, I find more than a few spuds notched by tiny teeth.

On the whole my garden is successful, considering the challenges I face (in this light, it is so successful I can pin a medal to my chest). My jumbo garlic grows to full size, as do my onions and often my parsnips and sometimes my turnips and occasionally my carrots, and so every autumn

I harvest some root crops in large enough quantities to store for winter. Every autumn I have jars of rhubarb jam, rhubarb syrup, and rhubarb sauce. I have jars of horse-radish sauce, spicy and not too hot. I have strings of peppers, some hot, some not, hanging from the rafters in the greenhouse, slowly turning red in the sun. So you see, bountiful or not, my harvest makes it all worthwhile in the end, all that frustration, all that failure, all that hoeing, weeding, and watering. It is worthwhile. In the end. Isn't it?

5
Foraging

In short, I am convinced, both by faith and experience, that to maintain one's self on this earth is not a hardship but a pastime, if we will live simply and wisely . . . . It is not necessary that a man should earn his living by the sweat of his brow, unless he sweats easier than I do.
—Henry David Thoreau

You don't have to eat wild mushrooms to enjoy them, any more than you have to eat wild birds to enjoy them. But if you are going to make a living off the land, it makes more sense to spend your time searching for mushrooms you will eat than searching for mushrooms you will not eat, mushrooms you will simply look at, study, identify.

Collecting mushrooms to eat is fun. I consider it my purest joy in my altogether joyous life. It's reasonably easy work. It's important work when beans and bread are our dinners, beans and bread being what us poor people eat.

On the other hand mushrooming for food is no more profitable, in terms of metabolic efficiency, than mushrooming for the heck of it. More calories are burned mushrooming than mushrooms provide when eaten, unless you eat them in gravy or in pizza or stuffed with sausage. Have you ever seen a recipe for plain mushrooms, plain old boiled mushrooms, no butter, no sauce? Of course not. So there you are.

As you might or might not know mushrooms are fleshy members of the fungi kingdom. As such they are related to many shifty enemies that have plagued human beings from day one.   Right now, as I write, fungi are eating Stew's rancid socks and the skin between his toes. They are eating my tent, the roots of my greenhouse seedlings, and my freshly baked bread. They are even eating our house, wood being wood after all, log walls or rotten trees. Therefore, to stretch the point, I find it fitting that we eat fungi, specifically, the fruiting bodies of fungi, in other words, mushrooms.

There are far too few mushrooms on Sawmill Creek that I consider delicious edibles. The name alone keeps me from considering stinkhorns as food (they smell like rotten meat with just a dash of sulpher gas). Along this same line, I might be tempted to eat mushrooms with such delicious and improbable names as tapioca, pretzel, red raspberry, carnival candy, scrambled eggs, and chocolate tubes, if I didn't know these mushrooms as "slimes," named individually for their appearance, not for their taste. In a similar manner, "jellies," those wonderfully weird mushrooms that look like ears, brains, and blobs, are named for their color (orange, apricot, and butter), not for their flavor. Indeed, some jellies are popular edibles even though their texture ranges from soft and gelatinous to stiff and rubbery and their taste, from rancid to flavorless.

To make mushroom collecting adventuresome there are many, far too many, poisonous species lurking out there. You betchum! Some of these mushrooms cause indigestion from mild to severe. Some send you soaring far into the stars. Some are so toxic my father warned me about them, my father who was also my doctor and the wisest man I have known. These mushrooms, when eaten in even minute quantities, cause a prolonged and hideous death. Am I scaring you? I'm scaring myself. Well consider this:

In 1988, an Oregon man, his wife, and a friend of theirs from Korea were innocently gathering chestnuts along the banks of the Columbia River. At some point they discovered the mushrooms that were destined to serve as a severe example to every mushroomer who is wont to identify species by guess or by group opinion.

These wild mushrooms growing beside the Columbia River looked sort of like the wild mushrooms the friend had eaten in Korea. As such, they were collected and served for dinner that night, laced with soy sauce. Two more people joined the ill-fated feast, bringing the victim count to five. "If they are poisonous," joked the wife, "we'll all go together." And indeed they did. They created a liver-transplant emergency for surgeons. Amazingly they survived in spite of having eaten *Amanita phalloides*, commonly called "death caps," one of the world's most deadly mushrooms. This is the kind of mistake my father warned me about (actually, he thought I was stupid to eat wild mushrooms at all). This kind of mistake gave rise to that time-honored truth: "There are *old* mushroom hunters and *bold* mushroom hunters, but there are no *old*, bold mushroom hunters."

In defiance of my father's great wisdom, I emerge from the meadows, the forests, the pungent green gloom of the aspen groves with pounds of mushrooms I plan to eat. If I am very careful, and believe me I try to be, this gentle sport of mushroom hunting need not turn into a death-defying feat. If I cannot tell for certain, without hesitation, that such and such a mushroom is what I think it is, then no matter how harmless it looks, how wonderfully mushroomy it smells, how it beckons, all but begs to be eaten, when in doubt I throw the sucker out (call this

Churchwell's Second Law). Should this mushroom I question have tiny teeth marks on the cap, I still throw it out. You see, certain wild animals, namely, squirrels, hares, and bears, for whom fungi function like salt licks, seem immune to the poisons that kill humans. And I never mess with mushrooms of the little brown kind found on cow pies and on suburban lawns. Be they edibles or hallucinogens or the kind of galerinas that cause renal failure, convulsions, coma, and death, they all look alike.

Wither mushrooms grow I go, albeit with caution at my heels, following me around like an unwanted dog. Through the late May leafage, I pursue mushrooms with considerable passion. In June, when nature hosts a mushroomfest, collecting becomes a basic part of my life. For most of a morning, then again, for most of an afternoon, I go along various roundabout routes, whatever takes my fancy.

When the green end of the spectrum dominates the landscape and a half-rainy mist swallows Van Horn Peak and the delicious vapor of wet earth, wet leaves, wet decay makes a weight in the air, the fruiting of morels kicks off this months-long celebration. *Morchella elata.* The golden syllables trip off my tongue as I go merrily, muddily through the rinsed brightness of the aspen groves. (I'm not going to tell you exactly which aspen groves. I don't want you getting there ahead of me next spring.) Here, morels await half-hidden in duff. With my pair of intent eyes, with a stopping, bending search, I quarter the ground below me. With little cries of ecstasy I greet every morel I find. Like old friends I recognize them, their black-ribbed beauty, their honey-combed caps. While my right hand plucks, my left hand holds the sack that keeps them safe.

When rainstorms come on like tropical downpours and the good earth is made even muddier, I bring morels home for dinner every day for an entire month. Stew always

makes a production out of their preparation, a little ceremony of stirring, carefully stirring, sniffing, tasting, constantly checking, smacking his lips. He has several ways of
serving them. The first night he might marinate them in
French dressing. The next night he might sauté them in
butter, not a moment overdone. The night after that he
might serve them swimming in a hearty brown gravy or
drowning in some thick fancy white sauce and ladled over
toast or skeins of skinny noodles or a hill of steamed
brown rice. What he doesn't serve for dinner I dry on
screened trays spread across the shelf of the greenhouse.
Stored in paper bags, morels last forever, or at least
through the winter. Simmered in Stew's secret spaghetti
sauce they rehydrate and taste freshly picked.

The timing of these rainstorms can't be counted on,
nor the duration. They can last for a few hours before moving on or they can settle in for days. Dressed in my neon
nylon storm-cruising rain suit, prepared for anything, I
explore within a larger and larger radius of the house, my
itinerary taking me nowhere in particular because mushrooms grow everywhere. The shade is cool, the grass dewy,
the sky full of puffy white clouds. I would be a fool to want
to live anywhere else.

I wade through meadows flooded green where fried
chicken mushrooms (*Lyophyllum descastes*) grow in large
grayish clumps, under and over each other, their caps
almost fused. When Stew slices them, sautés them in salad
oil, they taste just like, or almost like, or somewhat like
(depending on how meat-hungry we are) fried chicken.

Where the green swelling grasses are tinged with
wildflowers, mixed and matched, meadow mushrooms
(*Agaricus campestris*) grow in profusion, their caps smooth
and white, their gills a delicate pink underneath. There
are western lawn puffballs (*Vascellum pratense*) looking
for all the world like they just rolled off a country club fair-

way. By the way, all puffballs collected for the table should be as white and featureless as Wonder Bread. They become shriveled and yellow and bitter when they grow old (who of us doesn't). More important, each puffball should be sliced in half and each half closely inspected. If there is a faint outline of a cap and stem, this might not be a puffball at all, but the button stage of a deadly amanita, insidiously disguised as a harmless puffball. In nature we can trust only so far.

From the meadow I follow game trails through the lemony light of the fir forest, through a maze of crooked columns. The ground, a matrix of needles, mushrooms, and moss, feels springy to my feet, like I am walking on an inflated balloon. The air is fragrant with rot, with trees turning into earth as the earth is turning into trees. I am not so focused on finding mushrooms that I lose my senses, although I often lose the trails and I always lose track of time.

These fir forests I wander through are not old growth. That was all logged off in the 1940s. There was timber back then, slow growing, not big, but big enough. Then a few years ago the Challis National Forest logged these forests again, before the timber had time to grow back. As a result there are lots of spaces here bare of trees, untouched by the joy of spring, wasted spaces I visit for the sole purpose of collecting mushrooms, specifically, the giant puffballs (*Calvatia booniana*) larger than soccer balls. Just one makes several meals, each meal enjoyed afresh. Sliced into disks, coated with cornmeal, deep fried in fat, they smack deliciously of eggplant.

The Challis National Forest left a large strip of trees uncut, a fool 'em strip, to "preserve the visuals." Here I can still wander through a forest unspoiled. I can get lost in a world of nature's making. Coral mushrooms (*Ramariopsis kunzei*) grow here, delicate of taste, fragile of flesh, and looking more like what you would expect to find under the South Seas. There are boletes (*Suillus lakei*) that look like orange hamburger buns stuck on stalks. There are alcohol inkies (*Coprinus atramentarius*) irrigated by the secret springs that make of my shoes two wet sponges. Inkies I pick while they are still immature, while their egg-shaped caps are still tightly closed. Wait too late and their gills liquefy to a black

Western Painted Suillus
(Bolete family)

goo. Another thing. Friends don't let friends eat them drunk. Like the name suggests, alcohol inkies inactivate an enzyme in humans that detoxifies alcohol. Actually, it's the reaction to Stew's homebrew, not the mushroom itself, that causes toes to tingle, heads to ache, and our dinner guests to never return.

Another mushroom we no longer serve to guests, be they drunk or sober, are scaly pholiotas (*Pholiota squarrosa*). In times past I used to plot my whole day around collecting them, they were that good. Now I go a mile out of my way to avoid them. I mention this

Aspen Scaber Stalk
(Bolete family)

mushroom only in warning, to tell a tale that will have my dear dad turning in his grave–not, I am afraid, for the first time.

Several of our mushroom field guides (guides I have since tossed in the trash) list scaly pholiotas as "choice," meaning, they are not only edible but deliciously so. Indeed, even Roy and Chad agreed they were good. For two summers we ate them regularly without getting sick. Then one day, while mining mushrooms in an aspen grove I hit a mother lode of pholiotas growing in splendid golden bunches at the base of several elderly trees. That evening Stew baked them in a nettle-noodle casserole aptly named Mushroom Surprise. The trouble was, this dish was so good we stuffed ourselves to bursting.

Having polished off the casserole, a few minutes into dessert, our bellies began to gurgle and bubble with pholiota gas. We felt fluttery, uneasy, queasy, like the long night ahead might not go according to plan. "Mommmm, I think I'm gonna be sick." We all did. We all were. This was not just indigestion, or at least not the kind of indigestion that follows a Thanksgiving Day pigout. This was food poisoning. This was oh-lord-let-me-die abdominal cramps, upsurges and bowel purges that went like clockwork the whole night long.

Old mushroom hunters; *bold* mushroom hunters; no *old* bold mushroom hunters.

During the foggy days that followed as I lay in bed weak and mirthless I wondered what had gone so horribly wrong. How had I managed, in one stroke, to poison myself, my husband, my kiddies? When a sympathetic friend sent me a new field guide, Audubon's excellent field guide, the answer was made clear beyond the shadow of a doubt.

In fact the answer was twofold. In Audubon's guide it is written that thou shalt not eat large quantities of mush-

rooms at one sitting. Ever! It doesn't matter how often you
have eaten a particular mushroom. Mushrooms, in general, are indigestible. Then on page 717 there is this:
"Although the Scaly Pholiota was long regarded as edible,
it is now known to cause gastric discomfort in some people
within an hour after having been eaten." Gastric discomfort? This was more like convulsions, grand mal gastric
convulsions.

Needless to say there is nothing quite like pain to get
your attention. I learned my lesson. We all did. Oh sure, I
would still collect mushrooms when I could and eat them
although I shouldn't. But from now on I would follow reli-
giously all the mushrooming rules, every last one of them,
to the letter. I sounded so convincing I convinced Stew.
Unfortunately (or fortunately, depending upon your point
of view after reading this) I did not convince Roy and
Chad. Never would they eat rotty old mushrooms again,
wild or tame. Or as Chad put it, they would eat them
"when pigs fly."

The confounded part of foraging for wild foods is that
poisons also take a flowery form, albeit on Sawmill Creek
nothing as poisonous as mushrooms, nothing capable of
killing a forager. I am referring to death camas, of course,
and alpine buttercups, larkspur, Rocky Mountain irises,
lodgepole lupine, scarlet gilia . . . I could go on but you get
my gist.

Nevertheless, there is a place I know where more
plants grow edible than otherwise. There are wild Siberian
chives whose leaves, stems, and spicy pink blossoms gar-
nish our bean soups, bean burritos, three-bean salads,
bean and rice salads–in spring we eat lots of beans. There
are dandelion leaves that Stew steams in a pot and dandelion buds that pop into bloom while frying in the skillet.
When their full-blown flowers yellow the fields, Stew gath-

ers their petals for his kettles and brews a wine for sipping on cold winter nights (and other medicinal purposes).

The trail I take to this place I know, where the dandelions grow, is also the trail I take to the mailbox. This trail was never marked out or designed by Stew in any way. It was made by lots of busy hoofprints – pronghorns, deer, and elk taking a shortcut through our place. Little boys helped it along with their tennis shoes and bicycles. Now that the trail has fallen into disuse, or less use I should say, it is no longer sharply defined. Wild irises have softened its edges. In places it disappears under the various blues of lupines, gentians, and penstemons. The wildlife and I have to step high to get over the wind-thrown aspens, some of them thick as my waist and with woodpecker holes. They are too heavy for me to lift out of the way and I can't get Stew to cut them out of the way. He sees no purpose, with the boys and their bicycles gone.

The trail twists and turns with the creek, mighty Sawmill Creek. Halfway to the mailbox I stop in the pasture of private land fronting the west end of our property. Here Sawmill's original homestead stands in rotten ruins. This is the estate we share not presently but historically with the family who came before us, the Ghosts of Sawmill Creek. Though I am unrelated by blood I feel a kindred affection for this family. They were real people to me. They had been born, had worked and played and rejoiced and suffered and hoped and despaired. I feel like I know them, so often have I nosed around the junk they left behind, the rusted husks of vintage cars submerged in grass, the rusted remains of wagons and bed springs and cookstove parts, the petrified shoe soles and chug-alug jugs, laying as they had fallen.

In this estate, where the owners, the heirs, are absentee, a two-room log cabin stands wasting away with time, weather, neglect, smelling of dust mingled with the musk of disuse. Sunlight seeps between the logs in the walls where the old cement chinking fell out. The roof is wide open to the stars. Only the door, imbedded in dirt and stuck shut, discourages my unauthorized entry but not enough to keep me out. I feel a gust of ghostly scorn as I crawl through the paneless kitchen window. I hop down from what remains of the kitchen counter and find myself beside the stinging nettles and wild roses bedded where a dinner table must have stood. Gloves keep the nettle leaves from stinging my hands as I snip-snip here and snip-snip there. Steaming takes the sting out of the leaves. Pink rose petals perk up the dish.

Over the sound of my scissors the cabin echoes with emptiness. The past floats up around me. What happiness passed here long before my own? What sadness?

When the century was young this cabin was filled with the chatter and clutter of children. There were five kids living here. There was one bedroom. So where did they all sleep? Well in winter the four older kids boarded with families in town while they went to school. One of the surviving sisters now living in Montana told me this. In summer, she slept with her sister under the stars or under the storm clouds, in a wagon bed now entombed in the aspen grove where my mushrooms grow. Where my junkyard dandelions grow, her two brothers slept in the old car bodies no one ever cared enough about to haul away.

From the kitchen window I see our cabin looming with splendid jurisdiction, a cabin cared for, never to be forsaken, ghost-ridden, this cabin Stew and I so passionately love. But what if society claims our heirs like society claimed the heirs of my ghosts, Stew and I being what we are and Roy and Chad being what they are. What then? With no one around the chinking would fall out, the stars would come shining through, some stranger would come climbing through the kitchen window. But then, life is full of things you can do nothing about. Certainly, life is too short for brooding on old cabins. Time is too precious, I can't even spare ten minutes. So I shall simply believe everything will work out fine. It always does.

Not forever and always but for now, for today, I am the only stranger here. And in late summer I venture back to the aspen grove to collect currants. *Gooseberries!* The ghosts correct me. *Ribes.* My field guide corrects us all.

My field guide assures me there are twenty-five kinds of *Ribes* growing in the Rockies. Yet I find only a few kinds in Sawmill Canyon. There's that tasteless orange-colored kind growing on the bare mounds of dirt the Columbian ground squirrels have colonized. When I approach the colony, on the sneak, berry branches bend low with the considerable weight of these squirrels.

As these squirrels are very fond of berries, so the badger is very fond of squirrels, which has them on guard, standing tall on their hind feet, looking alertly about, their eyes bright and glittering. I wait for the alarm. It comes, piercing my ears. Branches spring upward with the communal dash to safety. The ground opens up, swallows every squirrel, those foraging on berries and those sunning themselves, scratching their fleas, bathing in dust. From burrows, dozens of unblinking eyes peep as I pass, curious as to what it was that scared them.

In several slot canyons branching off from Sawmill Creek, another kind of *Ribe* grows sweet and so plump they explode when I pluck them, staining my hands red. These canyons I speak of are too insignificant to be labeled on any map other than my mind. They are remote, so seldom visited, a person could break a leg or get lost, shout all week, and never be heard. Because Stew says he needs to know where I go, I have named these canyons, named

them for what I have found there besides *Ribes*. Rusty
Trap Canyon. Broken Snowshoe Canyon. Plenty Cattle
Canyon. Bear Canyon.

Bear Canyon. In my ten-odd years, my very odd years,
of beating about the bush in Sawmill Canyon, I have never
suffered from bearanoia, the jitters that all but bathed me
in adrenaline when I beat about the bush in Alaska's griz-
zly country. The black bears we have here are not threatening or aggressive, or I should say, they are not as threatening or as aggressive as grizzlies. Nevertheless, they are
just as unpredictable. You never know what they will do,
these black bears. And they are fast, faster than you can
think, faster than you can escape. They demand the
utmost respect and nowadays, ever since my misadventure, I plan to give them just that.

Oh, happy fool, I was working my way heedlessly up a
creek, or a trickle of water that passes for a creek in this
country. I was picking berries and I was feeling bear-like
picking berries. The bears were picking berries, too, judging from the big barefooted prints I kept passing and the
berry-colored scat, some of it cub-size, all of it steaming
fresh. I had one plastic freezer bag, crammed with berries,
cinched under my fannypack. I was so busy with a second
bag I didn't realize I was not alone. There, in the periph-
eral world just beyond the corners of my eyes, a small
blond cub went bouncing like a rubber ball into the berry
bushes in front of me. A little black ball of worry began
bouncing around in my head. Without a doubt there was a
sow nearby more than willing to kill for this cub. Playing
it safe, I slowly turned around and made my way up the
hillside away from the cub. But I didn't play it completely
safe. I have never been one to play it completely safe and
I saw no reason to do so now. I saw no reason why I could-
n't just sit down and watch this cute little cub for awhile.
So I sat down and watched in silence, completely hidden

by a thicket. And here came another cub, this one black as coal. And here came (oh wow!) the sow, half black, half blond, weirdest bear I ever saw. They came not from the forest but from a wildlife movie I could sit and watch to the end. My own private screening. I hugged myself in delight.

Hours might have gone by as I sat there spellbound, unblinking. Then my wondering eyes noticed something I should have noticed earlier, something that started the hairs moving on my head and the doves fluttering in my stomach. Although most of the berry bushes followed the creek, a few of them forked, angled up the hillside, and in fact made the very thicket I was sitting in. As I peered hard through the looped and tangled branches, stared hard through thorns and berries, my eyes watering with trying to focus, lo, I saw the bears moving slowly toward me. I had stayed too long. I had definitely stayed too long. Suddenly it seemed a good idea to get the heck out of there. But how? Stand and the sow would see me. Run and she'd catch me. Hide and she'd find me. Climb a tree and she'd pull me down. I wasn't exactly overwhelmed with options. I was in trouble. Big trouble. Now the sow had my undivided attention. You might say she had my attention by the throat. You can imagine what was running through my mind. Any minute now she would see me, charge me, grab me with her mighty paws, slash me with her needle-sharp claws, crush me in her dripping jaws, and call her cubs to dinner. That minute was almost here.

Sweat beaded on my forehead. She was close, too close, only a dozen yards away. And she didn't look as if she were about to lay down for her afternoon nap. Suddenly I found myself standing. I no longer looked like a bush. Or was it the scent of fear that gave me away. Her stare was straight and by no means loving. She was not going to fool with me, this bear. I raised the hairs on my head even higher to make myself look larger than life. I continued standing

there for a long time, a trembling long time, maybe a
minute. A long time. I did not, could not move. I stood . . .
rooted . . . to the ground.

In a furious whirlwind of maternal rage, the sow ran
her cubs up a tree. I remember hearing strange low-
pitched moans and being surprised they were coming from
me. She turned, charged me at a full gallop, only turning
away at the last minute. This is when something
approaching a miracle took place. My legs came unstuck. I
executed a half-torso twist. I ran. Full blast. Zoom. I
flashed through a screen of green that was the forest. I
flew over a blur of brown that was the ground. Until I
reached home I kept up this running motion, scattering
berries helter-skelter to the wind. If there had also been
the running sound of big bare feet in pursuit, I didn't hear
it for the terror pounding in my ears. But in fact had this
sow wanted to catch me she would have. Had she wanted
to kill me I'd be dead.

It was all over in a few deep breaths. Hours later I was
still gathering up the lose ends of me, still telling Stew the
story, first the outline, then the details, then more details.
Days later all I thought about, all I talked about, all I
dreamed about had to do with bears. For years I bored
everyone with this story. I bore them still, it so lingers in
my memory, scares me even there. But don't you get it?
That's the fun.

I have learned my lesson. Having learned it the hard
way I have learned it well. I no longer collect berries where
there are fresh signs of bears. I confine my collecting to the
forsaken estate where *Ribes* grow purple and mouth-puck-
ering tart. Their stems scratch like a cat but this doesn't
stop me from collecting enough for oatmeal, bran muffins,
and sourdough pancakes. On fruitful years collecting
berries becomes big business, time consuming, thought

provoking, snooze inducing, not everyone's idea of a devilish good time.

For reasons known only to nature, on years when berries are few, grasshoppers are aplenty. This is important to me not only because I am a gardener but because . . . well, this takes some telling.

Stew has always been fond of sneaking some unexpected ingredient into our meals. Then several years ago he read with near reverence a book about the early Shoshoni Indians, and he took a fancy to their diet, and he was eager to eat some of the items in their diet, and he talked me into this, talked me, on a dare, into trying several culinary experiments, the first of which he called Grasshopper Crunch.

When I agreed, reluctantly agreed, to eat grasshoppers, what I had in mind was simply to taste grasshoppers, one grasshopper, just one. Like the Shoshoni I would skewer this one grasshopper and roast it over a campfire, like a marshmallow. Stew had something different in mind. He made a huge butterfly net, then, since he is the cook and I am the collector, he bade me go forth and catch a bunch of grasshoppers. Well I tried to catch a bunch. Really I did. But my approach was always wrong, too noisy or something. The grasshoppers kept springing away from me, clattering like castanets. Hours later I returned home with only a dozen jumping in a jar.

Of course Stew was disappointed with the poor turnout. Nevertheless he was undaunted, darn it. He dumped the grasshoppers into a popcorn popper glittering with salad oil. He slammed down the lid before the grasshoppers could hop out. Shaking the pan once in a while to keep them from burning he cooked them alive, until they no longer hopped or popped.

We sat down to a table Stew had set elegantly, as if for company. He placed before us two salad plates filled with grasshoppers, six for him and six for me, or rather, the parts of grasshoppers, they had fallen apart–feelers, legs, wings, heads. They looked so totally alarming against the blue painted flowers of the plates I made Stew go first. He cleaned his plate, first with a salad fork, then with his fingers. They were delicious. They tasted like bacon. Now it was my turn. With a tweezer and a jumpy feeling, I stalked a grasshopper, or rather, I stalked a feeler, a twitching feeler, then a second twitching feeler, then six kicking legs, four shuttering wings, one bug-eyed head. Having thus tasted one whole grasshopper my part of the experiment was over and done.

Having eaten Grasshopper Crunch I was more than eager to skip Mock Rice Patties. To my astonishment I did eat them, and to my further astonishment they did taste like rice, and they looked like rice until you got up real close and saw how they looked more like something you would find in the forest, in the rottenest middle of the rottenest log. What Bits o' Beetle Soup looked like I'll leave to your imagination. It tasted – there's no polite way to say this – vile. Even Stew scrunched up his face and pronounced this one a "mistake."

There's just one more thing I want to say about all this, lest I disappear into the wilds of the truly bizarre. Just recently I read with a great deal of disbelief about a banquet put on by the New York Entomological Society. Its hundred or so members forked over forty-five dollars apiece for the privilege of dining on grasshoppers, grubs, beetles, and ants. This banquet proved so successful, the guest speaker was moved to predict that by the year 2000, grocery stores everywhere would be stocking their shelves with all kinds of insects. Well, having just eaten Stew's last worse experiment, something that would have put even entomologists off their appetites, I wouldn't bet the farm on this.

Alas, there comes a time when foraging for insects and foraging for anything else comes to an abrupt, awful end. It happens some warm, humming afternoon, when I am snipping greens or picking berries or picking mushrooms or simply sitting in the trembling green shade of aspens, wistfully worshipping the flower and birds, thinking half-formed thoughts of one thing or another or poised on the brink of some grand revelation. Time goes by. The creek goes by, this creek, as much to drink as to hear. There is nothing else, not the sound of a car, not the sound of a human voice.

Whoa, what's this? I do hear something else, faintly at first, coming closer and closer, growing louder and louder, trampling the song of the thrush, filling the air to bursting, and over it all and under it all and separating itself out, the frenzied yapping of cow dogs, the yodeling of cowboys, the pounding of horses, the thundering of cows, hundreds of cows, thousands of cows, hundreds of thousands of cows, all the cows in the world, making this one huge sound. With the noise fully upon me, I realize, with sinking heart, that every meadow, every aspen grove, every nook and cranny of every coyote canyon, all my secret laughing spots, will be filled with cows, cows trailing, cows trampling, cows chomping, cows defecating, cows camping in the creek. Whoopee-ti-yi-yo.

The thing is to let the cows have it. The thing is to just record it in a sad hopeless spirit. Let the others do the complaining, the green people. I have been an environmentalist for most of my adult life, and frankly, I am tired of arguing for my beliefs. With resignation, not outrage, I read how governmental regulations do not protect our natural resources, how the slow deterioration of our wild landscapes will continue indefinitely. I am powerless to prevent it. I no longer see myself as a force for change. I no

longer want to become involved. How many times do I
have to scream this at the empty air before Stew believes
me? I want to get on with my life, our life. I want to bury
my head in the good earth of Sawmill Canyon. But it's not
what I want that matters.

There was a time not too long ago, when our life here
was free, uncomplicated by Stew's radical environmental-
ism, his newfound passion for doing good. I don't even
understand his kind of dedication. He embraces one hopeless cause after another, trying to make the world—my
world—a better place to live. He spends all his spare time
and more than his spare money, money that is not there.
It never is for important things. What is worse, he defies
the customs and culture of Custer County, of which we are
members. There are narrow looks on the sidewalks of
Main Street, cold shoulders. Good people in our community, people we respect, people who used to smile when we
saw them, are convinced we are their enemy. We never
know from week to week who will snub us or refuse to do
business with us or threaten us with bodily harm, yes it
has come to that.

I think Stew and I are doing enough for the environ-
ment. We mulch. We recycle. We live simply and waste
nothing. We don't eat beef and we don't wear gold. And by
our example we encourage others to do as much. So I can't
understand, can't even imagine, why Stew wants to take
on the responsibility, the frustrating, unglamorous, thoroughly thankless work of saving the West.

Stew has changed and I have not (it's as if a third person is living with us). Whether this change is permanent
remains to be seen. I can't change him any more than I can
force open the petals of a wildflower. Surely this is just
something he has to go through, a search for personal ful-
fillment, a challenge he has to confront. He's a good man,
better than he knows, better than I am, much the better

person. He embraces all these lost causes, not for money, not for himself, but for better reasons. And me? You could say I epitomize the complacent environmentalist (you could say that, but I wouldn't like it). Well, however long it takes, I'll be waiting for Stew at the other end. Unless things go too far, beyond mending.

How Stew got involved with these green people lies as forgotten as I can forget it. It had something to do with the Sawmill Timber Sale, or I should say, with our battle to stop it, a battle that lasted for three long years, a lost battle I still agonize over today.

Black Monday we call it. Stew and I were putting the roof on the house, nailing down rafters, when we spotted a trio of uniformed strangers spraying-painting stripes on all the tree trunks beyond our fence. What are they *do*-ing, we finally wondered. Suddenly, like a slap upside the head, the clues clicked home. We realized for the first time, or allowed ourselves to think clearly for the first time, Sawmill's trees were about to come down.

It didn't matter that before buying our place we had checked these things out with the Challis Ranger District. No, we were told, Sawmill wasn't scheduled to be logged. It was roadless. The trees were small, worth more to wildlife than to the lumber mill in Salmon. What had changed? For one thing pressure to meet unrealistic timber quotas had filtered down to the district level. For another thing mill machinery had adapted to smaller trees. It had been forced to, all the real timber was gone.

So there we sat on the wall gawking in disbelief as the timber crew with their blue paint sentenced Sawmill's firs to their fate—brittle low-grade two-by-fours. Then to mark the sale's northern boundary, they painted orange stripes on our trees. Our trees! I leaped off the wall, went charging down the driveway, firing four-letter salvos over the heads of the crew. I intended to pummel them senseless with their own paint cans. And I would have too. But I felt this crushing hold on a vital part of my anatomy. "That's not the way to fight this thing." I always think Stew is shouting when I don't like what he is saying.

Okay then, let's tell the world about it, chain Chad to the bulldozer, splash it across the *New York Times*. Right. Another bad idea. We'd only make headlines in the *Messenger*. In the end we made no headlines at all. We fought it Stew's way.

For three years, for three frustrating years, we met once a month with the staff of the Challis National Forest, with their smarty-pants biologist, hydrologist, and silviculturist, sometimes at the sale site, sometimes in their offices, sometimes around our cozy kitchen table. They had been directed by those in command to Cooperate, Coordinate, Communicate with the Churchwells (the "Three Cs" as it is known within the agency). The hours drained away as these meetings fumbled on. We came to no solutions, no compromises, because right from the start this timber sale was a done deal. Politics. Down and dirty. We the people have very little control over our public lands, we, the little people.

The Sawmill Timber Sale was spawned by something the Challis National Forest called a "Notice of Decision" which was itself spawned by something called an "Environmental Assessment" in which the Forest Service assessed this and assessed that but never seriously considered the value of the forest left in its natural state, that is to say, uncut. The terms "highly unlikely" and "highly improbable" were not as convincing to us as to the Forest Service. So we went on fighting the sale with something called an "Appeal of Decision." Taking direction from the Wilderness Society, Stew and I typed our first appeal, fifty-plus pages detailing the damage, much of it irreparable, this timber sale would cause. When the Chief of the Forest

Service denied this appeal we typed another, a longer appeal, a sadder but wiser appeal.

To be sure, some of our concerns were selfish. After all, Sawmill Canyon is the center of all that counts with us. The sale would intrude into our sanctuary. It would shatter the mountain hush with high decibel noise–chainsaws, bulldozers, logging trucks. It would scar our vistas and by the Forest Service's own admission it would pollute our water supply. Indeed it has.

All this lather about saving Sawmill's trees got us a second denial. The Chief found "insignificant" every one of our concerns, everything we wrote, the lines that read like poetry, the wildlife that would also suffer from this sale:

> Pronghorns, porcupines, pileated woodpeckers, goshawks, mountain lions, martens, fishers, fox.
> Great gray owls, red squirrels, blue grouse, black bears, three-toed woodpeckers, northern pygmy owls, spotted frogs, showshoe hares.
> Vagrant shrews, least chipmunks, northern pocket gophers, big-eared bats, mule deer, pine grosbeaks, badgers, bobcats.

When this second appeal failed to stop the sale we took our case to court with the backing of a law firm that believed in our cause, believed it to be in the public's best interest, believed in it enough to work pro bono, for free. Churchwell versus the Rest of the United States. The result? Well, justice was blind. Or did justice merely look the other way? Or is justice even real, in the sense that killing a forest is real? In any case, for reasons beyond explaining, beyond reason, this federal judge, who had a heart two sizes too small, ruled in favor of the federal government. Case closed. After a three year delay the Sawmill Timber Sale proceeded as planned.

You might wonder how this could happen to us, the heroes of this book. Well for one thing we didn't have ten thousand dollars to appeal the judge's decision (as it was, we had to fork over three thousand dollars to cover our lawyers' expenses). And if you think about it long enough, hard enough, as I have for six years now, the rest is just as easily understood. We simply had no clout in court, no backing from the environmental heavyweights (like the Wilderness Society), all of whom were too busy attacking endangered species issues and Superfund sites and just generally trying to keep Congress from dismantling the gains of the past. What is even more disheartening is this. Had the judge ruled in our favor, our victory would have been a hollow one. Stopping this sale entirely was an impossible dream. The judge simply would have ordered the Forest Service to complete something called an "Environmental Impact Statement" (an EIS), meaning, more studies. More meetings. Another decision. Another appeal.

When it was over and done and lost, rotten with resentment, I packed it all away, the several cardboard boxes filled with reams and reams of type-written documents, documents that had ruined two summers for us. I packed away the Forest Service reports, thick as metropolitan phone books, but not nearly as interesting. And as I was packing everything away I realized there was no way we could have fought this thing and won. There is a message to me in this.

Into Sawmill Canyon the bulldozers came. Into the Taylor Mountain Roadless Area they came and left a new road five miles long. Chainsaws filled the air with the buzz of angry hornets. Logging trucks shattered the mountain hush. Angrily Stew and I packed the trailer and truck for an unscheduled migration, a return pilgrimage to our desert retreat. We left the next winter, too, until all Sawmill's blue-striped firs were stumps.

It was wrong to log Sawmill Canyon, wrong as in evil, unethical, improper, bad. But the thing is done. And in this imperfect world this kind of thing will keep on happening, to all of us. No place is sacred. Each of us will carry a loss, an offense against our special place, if not a clear-cut, then a subdivision, a shopping mall, a highway, always the highways.

The new logging road zigzags across one corner of our picture window (this is no more than I deserve for insisting on a view). Other than that, the fool 'em strip hides the sale from the house. The trick is to stay inside our fence. Whenever I climb the hillsides, any hillside, whenever I walk through the sale, my heart aches in a dozen small ways. Where once I saw a forest now I see a silent waste of stumps, standing like tombstones, and snags and slash and skid trails zigzagging through the stubble, and log landings and rusted cables and empty oil cans and more logging crud. Of course, the silviculturist at the Challis National Forest takes a different viewpoint. Where I see a forest that no longer functions, a bad haircut that will grow back inch by annual inch (if indeed, it grows back at all), she sees work done, a project finished, slash to burn, seedlings to plant, jobs for her crews, jobs for the small sawmill in Salmon, jobs, jobs, jobs, as if jobs justified everything. She sees future jobs and a new road she can extend a little further into the Taylor Mountain Roadless Area, on the theory that a little more roading and a little more logging will never be noticed. She sees another Sawmill Timber Sale ten years down the road and another one in thirty. I can see this too and I am so grateful I have lids for these eyes.

So the thing is to let the cows have it, to merely record it in a sad hopeless spirit.

6

The Lake

Time is but the stream I go a-fishing in.
– Henry David Thoreau

Even in the rawest light of an August noon the landscape is bewitching, stark and full of color at the same time. Below the serrated ranks of the skyline, below the gray thousand-foot walls of rock, below a no man's land of tenacious snow, giddy precipices, and crumbling tumbling talus, there are boulders strewn about, orange with lichen. At the bottom of this rocky wreck the lake spreads like blue satin then plunges off the edge of the earth. Only the flowery shoreline is orderly, arranged in colors so vivid they seem to stain the air around them. There are flowers galore, purple-pink shooting stars, lilac-purple penstemons, purple-blue lupines, violet-blue harebells, baby-blue forget-me-nots, deep-blue gentians, bright-yellow buttercups, pale-yellow columbine. There are pussytoes, storksbills, and yellow-throated monkey flowers that look comically unfloral when seen close up, and elephantheads that look like little pink elephant faces complete with oversized ears and up-curving trumpeting trunks.

The days of August are lazy days for me, the time after planting and the time before harvesting. The garden grows with or without my help, whether I stay home or not. With Stew always gone, winding up little matters in Ketchum, in Boise, in Missoula, there is no point in my staying home.

His week-long absences are a privation for me. Without Stew, home is no longer home.

So I go to these lakes in the White Clouds, most often to Lonesome lake, a lake I used to share with Stew and the boys, then with just Stew. Now I go alone and am content to be alone. Well, not really content. And not really alone. Cujo is with me. Certainly there are bad moments when I sit before the campfire and realize Stew is no longer on the other side. I try not to think unlovingly of him at times like this.

I started backpacking alone about the time Stew started trying to save the West. All summer I had planned backpacking trips we never took. I foresaw all the agonizing loneliness of the rest of the summer—even, vaguely, of the rest of my life. "You are always welcome to come with me." Stew was bending over his suitcase with folded sweaters and slacks. He didn't sound like he really welcomed my coming at all. What would I do caged in a hotel room, riding out his work sessions, chewing my nails. I am not one to wait with my knitting. My days are too numbered to be spent waiting.

It made more sense to have Stew drop me off at the trailhead on his way out of town. This met with his approval, his entire approval. He thought I needed to keep testing the unknown, my independence, my life alone. See, there was this part of me that wanted a big strong man to take care of me. And there was another part of me that hated that part of me.

"What if you get lost?" Fear weighed heavily on my mother's mind. I get lost easily. If you were to drop Stew and me in the woods, he would find his way home and I would crawl up in a hollow log and just die. I get lost in shopping malls and parking lots. I get lost in Sawmill Canyon, or not lost exactly. Let's just say that sometimes I find myself in a forest I recognize only as unfamiliar.

My mother thought it unwise to backpack alone. I thought it was unwise, too, but it was necessary. I really, really wanted to do it. Or rather, I wanted to have done it, for the good of my soul . . . or something. What if I get lost? I had about four separate answers to this, but they all failed me. Obviously, I would have to deal with it in a manly way even though I didn't feel manly, didn't feel equal to the challenge. Nevertheless, if I faced my fear of getting lost, voluntarily, and triumphed, I would forever have power over it.

The air of preparation permeated the house, Stew packing, me packing with some urgent purpose of my own, all the while wondering what I thought I was doing. I can talk myself into these things as easily as I can talk myself out. I got out the topo maps and spread them across the living room floor. Behold: 20,000 square miles of wilderness—the Sawtooths, the White Clouds, the Pioneers, the Boulders, the Bighorn Crags, all within reasonable driving distance from Sawmill Creek. A dazzling variety of possibilities presented themselves to me, the most outstanding of which were the subalpine lakes. But which lake? Like jewels they chained across the maps. I walked my fingers from one lake to the next. Skyhigh, Tip Top, Tin Cup, Hourglass, Gooseneck, Pothole, Crater, Noisy, Quiet, Lonesome, Lost. I let Cujo decide. Ah yes. Of course. Lost Lake. That's where we would go. We would make the best of it without Stew. We would have fun. Repeat after me. We would have fun.

I was actually on the verge of getting into this trip, bending over my backpack, stuffing the pockets with a week's worth of self-sufficiency, some of it essential for back country survival, some of it not. I can never decide what to take and what to leave behind so I ended up packing it all: first aid kit, sewing kit, mess kit, patch kit, compass, maps, flashlight, toilet paper, matches, fly rod and reel, daypack for hiking, binoculars for birding, field guides for flowers, for mushrooms, for butterflies, a paperback novel (my personal rainy-day kit), camera, lenses, film, and my entire wardrobe of wool. I was not overly concerned with saving space (I didn't saw the handle off my toothbrush or take the cardboard core out of the toilet paper roll) which is why not everything rode tidily inside. I had to lash my mummy bag to the bottom of the pack and to the top, my primeval shelter, the one-person-plus-dog-instant-up tent I mail-ordered on impulse a few weeks before. I strapped on any which way my air mattress, my sneakers, my coat, a water bottle, a billycan and a frying pan blackened by countless family campfires. Cujo carried the food, twenty-five pounds worth of kibbles, rolled oats, nuts, sunflower seeds, homemade elk jerky, elk sausage, and almost-instant soup.

The trailhead was at road's end. Here Stew and I synchronized our watches. We saddled Cujo while he boinged into the air, his tongue flapping happily. Come on! Come on! Then we saddled me. Stew held my forty-pound pack braced against his knees while I struggled my way into the shoulder straps. I cinched the belt tight, until it pinched my fleshy hips. Groan. Maybe I should just go on back home, lay around and knit instead.

Stew was running late, rushed. "Well," he said, "have a good time. Don't get lost."

"I will. I won't." I turned as if to go, then turned again, watched Stew drive away, Stew, my only friend, my only way home. Billows of dust ran after him. I ran after him. Wait! Wait! Too late. He was gone. Loneliness at the trailhead. He wouldn't be back to pick me up for one hundred and sixty-eight hours, but who was counting. I wrinkled my nose, fussed with my bifocals. "Courage," I told Cujo. "Courage!"

Getting to this lake was not easy. Lacking wings, there

was only one good way to go. And the thigh-burning push to the ridge was just for starters.

There were forests insane with insects, mosquitoes biting me with carefree abandon. I tried to wave them away. If only the breeze would stiffen up. Instead it died to the merest puff. *Slap. Slap. Slap.*

There were creeks to cross high as my knees, icy with snowmelt. My mother would be so disappointed if I drowned.

There was snow up to my wazoo.

There were waterfalls and tall vicious walls of rock where the trail stood on end in narrow-gauge zigzags and got even longer as I huff my way up, gravity collecting in my legs, my legs working like pistons, my lungs working hard to keep me alive. Fishing pole leading the way, I climbed, took a moment's rest, climbed some more. I entertained myself with worries. Did I turn off the burner? Did I lock the back door? Did I even *close* the back door? This was good for another mile or so.

At last, the lake, at the end of the world. I didn't know how I got there but I got there. With a heavy sigh I unsaddled myself, then Cujo. Unburdened, he lifted his hind leg, did so freely, aiming his golden jet on the trees until he ran dry. I dropped down on a living carpet of the softest moss, and, upon closer inspection, some freshly deposited elk pellets. I shucked off my boots, eased into my sneakers, and surrendered myself to the sun still high in the great blue stretch of sky, a sky I had all to myself. No other campers. Or none visable.

I don't mean to be talking old here but my bones felt old and weak from overuse. My legs had given up. My feet were no happier. I needed a long peaceful rest. It was early afternoon, the sun plenty high in the sky. There was lots of daylight left, time to fetch water and firewood, to set up camp, the tent over there under the trees where the ground was level and bare of vegetation, the kitchen over there in the open with everything in easy reach. Thanks to the long light of these northern summers there was plenty of time. It was not going to rain. It never rains real rain. This is where the sky was supposed to suddenly turn black and thunder clap.

I never knew how the afternoon got away from me but it did. It just seemed to float off like the butterflies I sat watching as they fluttered around prettily, their wings slowly opening and closing above the blooms. I watched the sun move across the sky, already lower on the horizon, already moving away, toward night. So here I was–the big chill rolling into camp, the lights going out–rushing around staking down tent walls, inflating air mattress, fluffing mummy bag, pitching into the tent everything I needed for the night, fetching water, fetching firewood, building a campfire ring, building a campfire, boiling water for soup, a veritable windstorm of activity.

Water boiling, I stirred in two handfuls of almost-instant soup. Almost instantly the noodles were soft, the sliced vegetables plump, the garlicky sausage flavoring the air. Comfortably couched on my air mattress placed well within the campfire's circle of warmth, light, and security, I hunched over my Sierra cup and enthusiastically, unshamefully slurped. I realized that the only thing better than having a place like this all to myself is having it all to myself with Stew.

After dinner there was nothing to do but look at the lake, the rippled images on the lake, the mirrored moon, the two lines of pines, one real, one reflected. Having looked at the lake for a respectable amount of time I watched the stars come on one by one, each one in its own time. I watched the campfire, my ecologically incorrect campfire, the sticks shifting slightly as the flames took them, the flames tumbling upon themselves, a cascade of live coals. A glowing spark shot out. Ouch! And another. *Sssssss*. Patch time.

Too tired to go to bed, I sat beside the fire, watching the flames flicker so low they no longer kept me warm. I had not fetched enough firewood while it was daylight and I sure wasn't going into the forest when it was full of hulking shadows. I felt the prickle of yellow-eyed surveillance on my back. I went into the tent and whistled in Cujo, his business with trees over and done. I took comfort running my fingers through the deep soft nap of his neck. Cocooned inside my mummy, by flashlight I read myself sleepy.

Sleepy I was but sleep didn't come easily. The ground beneath the tent wasn't as level, as bare of vegetation as I had supposed. Having popped my air mattress, having left my patch kit at home, I had to arrange my bones around roots and rocks. For a long time I lay unsleeping, listening to the night noises, a crunch in the pine needles, a whisper of wings, a woeful wailing from the ridge. I heard the distant and nearby falling of rocks, small avalanches, big avalanches. Had I pitched my tent entirely out of harm's way? In the dark, an unsettling vision played across my eyes. I saw all those gnarly trees standing above me at the crumbling edge of life, rooted in rock, grappling, grabbing at thin air, listing over at crazy angles, their naked arms rising eerily in a kind of stark terror.

I began to doze, not without thinking, "I am beginning to doze." By notches I dropped into a shallow fitful sleep, barely touching bottom before I would wake again, with a jerk. There were shadows playing across the tent. The moon, having pierced the canopy of evergreens, beamed through the tent like someone's flashlight. There was the sharp bark of a fox. There was—omigod—what was that! Something or some*one* was walking around out there. I was not prepared for this, not armed, not trained, not brave. I whipped zippers open, my bag, the tent. I dashed outside. The darkness leaped at me like a living thing, utterly eerie. I peered into the night and saw the food bag still hanging undisturbed from a tree. I saw nothing else, not a soul, not a creature, not even a mouse.

I listened to my watch ticking toward midnight, the hour when nothing good ever happens. Snuggling up to my knees I slept one eye at a time while the bears went prowling and the wind went howling, whipping the grass into itself, each gust bellying the tent walls, cracking them like gunshots. The clouds blackened the moon. Thunder clapped, boomed across the sky. A hundred licks of lightning flashed in the distance then directly overhead, lighting the clouds theatrically. I listened as heavy sullen raindrops splattered the tent, drops the size of nickles. Rain, real rain, hissing sluicing roaring rain. My hand reached out for Cujo. I worked my fingers across his forehead, around his ears, through the warm thick reassuring fur of his chest. Still I was afraid, afraid I might drown, afraid my wilderness skills would be tested to the limit, afraid I would have to cope with days of spirit-drenching drizzle, with days of hideous confinement in this green nylon cave. I had brought along only one book. *Singing Guns.*

Dawn came, dark with overcast. Noon came dissolved in drizzle. The tent smelled like the winter den of some big hairy animal. It was a jungle of humidity, the walls sodden, sagging dismally, coming toward me in suffocating wet sheets. Everything was soaked, or if not soaked, then wet, myself included. It was still raining with a spiteful persistence. It would keep coming down whether I wanted it to or not. But surely at some point it would stop, it always did, I only had to wait.

Meanwhile, cooking over a campfire was inconvenient, if not downright impossible. So I chewed on elk jerky for breakfast and again for lunch. Only my need for coffee drove me outside, dashing through the dripping forest, ripping lichen, twigs, and sticks from beneath boughs sagging with saturation. I was back in camp in, oh, three minutes. Somehow I managed to get the kindling lit. It took so many matches. I coaxed the kindling into steamy smoke and fueled the smoke with more sticks.

Back inside the tent I wrapped my hands around a cup of coffee. As if on cue the rain lightened up, stopped. Coffee no longer had any meaning. I went sloshing out the tent and into a world newly made. A ruby-crowned kinglet greeted me with a furious warble of joy. A clean white fog snuggled itself around the peaks, slinked across the landscape, thickened and thinned as the sun reasserted itself. The lake was a blur. Then it cleared in the sudden sun. The peaks appeared above the clouds and the snowcaps above them and my spirits lifted in response. My tent steamed dry, and my sleeping bag strung on a line between two pines. I roasted my wet socks over the smoky campfire. All was well. The world would always be like this. If I could just get through the nights and if the gods of real rain didn't spoil my great plans the next hundred and forty-four hours would be pure pleasure.

That afternoon and the next one and the next, I climbed above one lake to the next one and the next. I hung out around the ten-thousand-foot contours where the land lifted mightiest and miles of mountains rose-purple with heather in every direction stretched to the edge. The air was icy, the lake, tiled with ice. The crystals collided in the breeze, filling the amphitheater with the music of wind chimes.

In this one lake I will leave unnamed the trout grew so fat on freshwater shrimp they had to be halved to fit in my pan. Just hooking a fish like this is worth a year's happiness to some people I know. Out from under a chunk of ice swam just such a fish. With a bubble and a "blurp" it sucked up something with wings. A great rainbow of a smile spread across my face. Oh, I can already taste your sweet pink flesh. I scrambled to assemble my rod and reel. My fingers danced through the fly box searching for something winged. I–woops–spilled the fly box and all my feathered hooks went fluttering to the ground. I collected my wits. I collected my flies. Hurry. Too late. The fish was gone. Scanning the muddy landscape of the lake bottom, I saw another fishy movement. I prepared to cast. *Woosh.* My bright yellow line sliced the air effortlessly, no stops, no jerks. My fly dropped–*splash*–in front of me, right on top of the fish. The fish rushed off to pass the word around the lake. "Watch out for the bogus black gnat with the loose thread."

Being a bit larger than life, Stew, ace angler, can cast successfully, on the whole, shooting 60 feet of fly line into a 15-knot headwind, whipping it around, floating his fly down softly, here and here and here, exactly where he wants it. I always let myself be impressed for precisely ten seconds.

Now me, I cast as if I were tossing a skillet overhead, or so Stew tells me. He feels compelled to coach me. "Don't swing your elbow out like that. You're coming back too far. Now you've got it. Uh oh."

As you might have guessed I make my own flies. For my Itsy-bitsies I wrap a number eighteen hook with deer hair and ostrich herl. For my Teeny-weenies I use a little dab of spit to dub on some fur, the fur being that of a road-killed house cat. As you also might have guessed my flies don't match the hatch. They would never be sold in a sporting goods store. They are too crude, too odd, anyway, too something. But they sure fool fish, to a most extraordinary degree.

With the breeze at my back, lap-lap-lapping waves against the shore, I peeled out line, waved my long wand, aimed it, fired. And hooked the pine tree directly behind me. After my tenth sloppy cast I managed to get my Teeny-weenie way the heck out there. What I had ahead of me was a long wait. Giving in to the pull of gravity I sat down. I stopped thinking. Sometimes I do this when I am fishing. I let my mind wander around in idiotic idleness. My chin dropped to my shirt. I snoozed in the shade of my cap.

Not soft as you please but suddenly–BAM–something clobbered my fly. My rod tip plunged as a full-figured fish broke the surface of the lake with a great gut-wrenching leap. Grimly I hung on while the fish shot toward the opposite shore, ripping line off my reel, the drag screaming, my rod bent double. Across the lake and back, with no rest stops, and I'm trying to retrieve my line, trying to keep it tense, looping and snarling the slack at my feet.

In a business-like manner I beached the fish, without a net. It was a male cutthroat, well over twice as big as the next biggest trout I ever caught, before or since, a beautiful fish, a wonderful fish, a frantic, flapping, slippery fish. I pressed it against the ground with one hand. With the other hand I banged it on the head with a rock. The fish went still. Eyes bright and clear with panic dimmed in death. I slit him from the vent on his satiny belly to his big underslung jaw. I stripped out the guts and gills, all in one piece. I washed the fish in the lake. Now it looked more like dinner.

Since there was no need to fish anymore that day, I cased my fly rod. I still had a whole afternoon ahead of me, an afternoon full of possibilities. I might just sprout wings and fly.

Through the rest of the week I moved languidly through long days of sweet drenching sunshine. I went looking for perfect sunsets and for lakes still unknown to me, lakes whose names I didn't know, if, indeed, they had names at all, more lakes than you could shake a map at. I went and saw what I could see, knowing I would never come close to seeing it all. Then, for my roaring appetite I ate the fish I hated to kill.

Just when I was falling into the rhythms of camp life, just when things were shifting from the edge of loneliness to the edge of real fun, I remembered I had something to do, or was it somewhere I had to go, or someone I had to meet. Must be Stew I decided. Part of me was rehearsing our reunion all the way down the trail, although there was no need to plan what to say, it would all be easy seeing him again.

"I had all the fun a body can have." I wrote my mother a five-page letter chronicling my trip. "It was wonderful, that's what it was. The fishing. The long hikes. The solitude. The sunsets. You wouldn't believe the sunsets. And I even took time out to get good and properly lost."

7
The Hunt

I have no doubt that it is a part of the destiny of the human race, in its gradual improvement, to leave off eating animals, as surely as the savage tribes have left off eating each other.
–Henry David Thoreau

Van Horn Meadows.

September 10: Lord what a morning! It's a glorious red from the turned leaves of wild geraniums. It's green with moss, brown with bracken, and yellow with sunflowers, the last flowers of the season. The golden seed-tasseled grasses are long and lush, brazen against the dark backdrop of pines. There's a Christmas smell everywhere, a smell I breathe as deeply as I breathe air. The sun, summer warm, has stripped me to tee shirt and shorts. I want every pore open to this sun. I want only to lie here plucking grass with my toes, waiting for something to happen – or not to happen. Idleness perhaps, but time has been worse spent.

While I am lounging, Stew is sneaking his way through the forests, like an elk, dressed like an elk, dressed in elk, in Jim Bridger britches so stiff with dried blood and elk guts they can stand up on their own. It goes without saying he talks like an elk with the bugle he made from a plastic sawed-off baseball bat, the diaphragm cut from a condom. And he surely smells like an elk with fresh elk pellets mashed, rubbed all over his arms. That's about as far as my analogy can stretch.

It's September and September is bow hunting season and Stew is a bow hunter. He relates to bow hunting more than he relates to anything else in life. Believe me. I've spent a lot of time lounging, figuring these things out.

In bow hunting, as in almost everything else he does, Stew is bound to tradition. Like a mountain man, his beard is wild and furious, his look, lean and hungry. The recurve bow he carries is very much like the bows the early Shoshonis carried, a simple weapon, graceful, light as a feather.

Stew bolts to this simple weapon a quiverful of arrows fletched with turkey feathers and tipped with two-bladed broadheads sharp enough for shaving, arrowheads no Indian ever used. Again breaking with tradition, he bolts to this simple weapon a spool wound thick with tracker string, a half-mile length of dental floss that glows fluorescent orange. He keeps a spare spool of tracker string in his tackle box, and a spare bowstring, a bow stringer, a tin of string wax, and string silencers. There are more string things in there and arrow things whose purposes I can only guess at but whose importance to the bow hunter I will concede.

Stew hunts hard. Chugging up hillsides, stalking elk along a web-work of game trails, he covers a lot of ground, over three hundred miles a season by his estimate. To get himself in shape for this he lifts weights until his muscles are as hard as the bones they are strung on. Having let myself become flabbed beyond redemption, I find his fabulous abs quite inspiring. So are his quads made mighty from running up and down Morgan Creek Road, ten miles every other day. Motorists pass him and have to wonder,

Where did this guy come from? Where is his car? What's chasing him anyway?

I don't get myself in shape for hunting because I don't hunt, although I did once, just once. It was easily the most hideous experience of my life, as difficult to accept as it is impossible to forget.

The little buck I shot wasn't even looking at me, didn't know I was there across the canyon, watching him through the rifle scope as he bent his head gracefully and nibbled at a shrub. With Stew's coaching I took aim and put a bullet through his lungs. He swooned, folded up, fell, mortally wounded but still alive. Now he was looking for me across the canyon, looking for me.

I was not prepared for this, the roaring confusion, the profound sorrow I felt. Down one side of the canyon, down a minefield of talus, boulders, bushes, I slid, skidded, stumbled, my face streaming tears. I clambered up the other side, desperately needing to reach this deer, to finish the job, to put out the pain I saw staring out those huge soulful eyes. Even as his lifeblood was running redly, steadily out, I sat dangerously on his back, sawing my knife across his throat, or trying to. I watched the knife and my hand go blurry from helpless, angry tears. I hadn't even nick the hide when Stew showed up, shoved me aside, took knife in hand, and ended the misery for us all.

So there you have it, why I don't hunt, why I am happy to stay in camp, why Stew is happy to have me stay in camp. And since I will be staying in camp it is my job to keep the campfire burning, the coffee hot, and the soup simmering (Stew usually returns to camp around noon). Oh, and I'm supposed to run off the mad biting bears. How would I do that? Well I would stare the bear in the face, without blinking, and shout, "YAAAH! HAAH! WOOHA! SCRAM! " That should do it don't you think?

Van Horn Meadows.

September 13: There's a wind from the west blowing hot as if off a desert. There's smoke that has risen from nearly nothing this morning to a fairly large something this afternoon, a choking throat-burning smoke, a smoke that makes the sun look like a harvest moon. Orange moon, orange light, orange smoke. In these mountains you can never tell where a forest fire is, how far away it is, a hundred miles or the next canyon over. Even now Stew and I might be trapped, about to be sucked up in a cyclone of flames.

After hunting all morning on the ridge, Stew returns to camp and assures me the fire is hundreds of miles away, nothing to worry about, we will not awaken in the night to a sky full of burning branches. With a weary groan he sits himself down on a tree stump drawn close to the campfire, his shoulders hunched with fatigue. He ladles soup into his cup, and while working on it, as is his custom, he tells me about his morning hunt, a hunting story he enjoys as much as the hunt. His rich baritone conjures up scenes I can almost see: pursuits, missed opportunities, and wonderful incredible ironies. He glances at me now and then for some sign of interest, encouragement, appreciation, all of which duly comes. He so whets my appetite for adventure I want to go on his next hunt, follow along, not participating in the hunt, even as an onlooker, but just lagging behind like a dog. I have done this twice already, gone on a hunt. Unlike Stew, I do not enjoy telling these hunting stories any more than I enjoyed the hunts. Nevertheless, this will not stop me from telling them here.

Why is it that some people who possess a watch are possessed by it. "It is now 0500 hours. Move it! Rise and Shine and Greet the Dawn." This, coming so close to my ear, brought me up from the depths of sleep. Then I got a bark shoved down my ear, foul dog breath and all. A crushing weight on my chest brought me snarling out the tent and into the large unexplored realm of predawn dark. I was handed a cup of coffee, thick, dark purple, no milk, no sugar, so strong it pasted my eyelids permanently open. I was handed a cup of oatmeal, lumpy, gray, no milk, no sugar. Already I was regretting this business but I could think of no graceful way out.

Things got worse. Stew blackened my face with a cold lump of charcoal, a great streak here across my forehead, another down my nose, two more beneath my eyes. This would dull my shine he said when the steady complaining of my voice would not stop. To blend me with shadows, I was gotten into a pair of Stew's old Vietnam War jungle fatigues, the pants rolled up at the cuffs, the waist cinched tight with a rope. To mask my human scent, my arms, from elbow to wrist, were smeared with globs of elk pellets, dung, excrement. Wasn't this terrific, all I could have asked for? I frowned. Stew took a big sniff of me and smiled. He stepped back to further assess me by campfire light. He smiled a bigger smile, a self-satisfied smile. Yes, I would do. And so I found myself stumbling through the gates of dawn, camouflaged in jungle leaves, smelling gamy as a zoo, my flashlight beam wobbling before me.

The morning was rising rapidly on the east side of the ridge. I could hear Cujo's howling complaints at being tied in camp, at having wound himself around the tree trunk so tightly he couldn't move. I was being led at a spanking pace, an uphill climb, a downhill slide, into the forest and through the forest, now at a hunter's pace. One step, look everywhere. Another step, look everywhere, Stew alert in every whisker. Every once in a while I allowed myself a wide vocal yawn, to make my point, as every once in a while Stew stopped and blew through his baseball bat a melodic "eeedleoop" then a "yuck, yuck, yuck." Although I listened hard I didn't hear an answer. Then I did.

I had been thinking how this wasn't fun, not even a little bit, how I had learned my lesson, I would never do this again, ever, when suddenly the air swelled and throbbed with a bellow from what had to be, oh boy, the biggest baddest bull in the Rockies. Stew raised his baseball bat and answered the challenge.

We advanced toward the bull, and as we advanced, back and forth it went, the bull, the bat, the bull, the bat, until we reached the perimeter of the bull's fight threshold. At this point the Commander of the Forest, fired with desire, supercharged with power, conscious of his strength, filled his lungs and poured forth a tremendous guttural roar that faded and dropped to several savage grunts. The bull answered back.

Stew said he wanted to go on alone. I found a patch of bare ground and sat. I was supposed to keep myself handy and invisible. "Just be quiet. You got that?" I nodded, I did. But later on I wished he had given me more detailed instructions.

The sun rose higher, higher. Hour after lonely hour I sat. And sat. And sat, patiently at first, then impatiently, my legs stiff with sitting cross-legged on the ground, my jaws cracking with yawns, yawning, this time quite naturally. I begged myself to sit there a little longer. And I sat there a little longer until I felt I had to complain. I just needed one more minute to think. I thought. I stood. Stew hadn't said not to, so, obeying an impulse, I followed his tracks into the forest, an oldish woman talking to herself in the gloom. I followed fresh elk tracks deeper into the forest. Where the heck was I anyway? Quick now. What do you do when you panic? I, for one, begin yodeling, frantically. This time I really poured my soul into it, my voice ricocheting off the trees, tears rolling down my cheeks as I

strained my ears for Stew's reassuring shout. Not one
human sound came back to me. But I did hear what sounded like a considerable body of hoofed animals put suddenly in motion. Oh great! Stew would never understand this,
not even a little bit. And there he was, standing in the middle of a dusty trail, as if on display. I walked into his plain
view but he didn't see me. He wouldn't see me. He active-
ly refused to see me. He would have torn his hair out had
he any hair to spare.

You would think, by mutual agreement, I would spend
the rest of my days in camp, lashed to a tree with Cujo. You
would think it highly unlikely, no, highly absurd, I would
ever want to go hunting again. But a few years later I did
want to. I went.

Before I begin this next story Stew has asked me to
run something by you. See, these big bulls he bugles, these
strong healthy bulls that come so readily, so reliably to his
bidding, well, he doesn't kill them. He lets them get on
with the important business of begetting strong healthy
calves. As I understand it, he bugles them only to locate
the herds. He kills for meat. Period.

So: The morning of this second hunt went pretty much
like the morning of the first hunt. This time I had Cujo for
company. For hours we sat, fidgeting, wondering. And
where was Stew? He was stalking with pig-headed determination a she-elk. Once Stew gets on a hot trail there's no
stopping him. At the very lowest bottom of a deep canyon,
a rocky gash of a canyon, he killed this cow, without ever
stopping for even a moment to consider how the bloody
hell we would get the carcass up and out of that canyon
before dark.

I've said this before but it bears repeating. Stew usually supposes he can get something done in less time that
it actually takes him. He is always full of errant enthusiasm. He creates such suspense he arouses me to states of

worry. Indeed, that was the case here. We were caught in the dark, come early under an overcast sky. With the carcass only halfway up the canyon, we had no choice but to camp right on the spot. (Right where? Right here.) Our camp amenities, tent, sleeping bags, flashlights, were miles away. All we had were the clothes we stood in, sweaty, bloody, stinking with the essence of elk.

Stew is healthy and strong and does not believe in death from exposure. With precious few exceptions, he can't distinguish between adventure and misadventure. What is fun for him is misery for me. He seemed immensely pleased by our circumstances. With unbearable enthusiasm he announced, after digging deep in his pockets, "We have matches." We had Fire, if nothing else. We had Warmth and Light and a Feast of Meat, the still-warm flesh of his victim. Also we would have the satisfaction, the heroic satisfaction, of enduring the ordeal looming ahead of us in this cold black canyon. All we needed now was for it to rain. And that it did.

It was a dark and stormy night. It was not night as I knew it or ever dreamed it could be. To begin with there was an interesting half hour when we sat cross-legged, slanted on the slope, hunched against a drizzle that sizzled in the campfire. Above the sweet smoke we held willow branches strung with chunks of dead elk, charring each chunk to perfection. Fat fed the coals in tiny explosions of flame. Fat streamed down our chins as in our hunger we tore into the meat with our teeth, eating gross amounts, wiping our mouths with the back of our hands, wiping our hands across the legs of our pants, our faces sweating with the work of overeating. Still we went on eating, gorging ourselves to our cubic capacity, as if we were trying to satisfy some primeval urge.

The clouds parted and in the west the moon rose eerily and so huge it felt warm. Buttons unfastened, belt slackened to insure good digestion, I sat stunned, sleepy, full of dead elk. After brushing my teeth, with my fingers, I sat crosslegged beside the fire, surviving the night, my hands holding up my head grown heavy. Stew hadn't said which one of us had to stay awake to feed the fire, and I didn't think he was ever going to say who, so I simply closed my eyes. I kept jerking awake to find my chin on my chest, my neck stretched to the limit, kinked. I laid down beside Cujo and tried to sleep, first with my ear against the pine needles and dirt, then on my back, then curled up on my side, my hands palm against palm pillowing my head. For about an hour I lay like this, slanted on the slope, turning my hot side outside, my cold side fireside, trying to get myself warm by remembering what warm was like. I couldn't concentrate on anything but me trying to get warm.

Had I slept? I might have, I felt less sleepy anyway. I sat up and began a heroic attempt at entertainment, telling Stew my life story from beginning to end, adding nothing he hadn't heard before. When I finished, Stew told me his life story, and again I saw how everything in his past contributed to the making of this man sitting before me, this man who was slowly talking himself into such a state of nostalgia his eyes became dreamy. He gazed into the fire and beyond it into his past, a past I played no part in. I lost him for about an hour, his private thoughts staying private to himself. It didn't matter. That was another hour gone by. And with every hour that went by there was one less hour to go.

Clouds streamed across the moon and the moon seemed to move visibly toward the western side of the sky. When Stew was through brooding on the flames, he suggested we eat again just for something to do, and we did that, ate. Having eaten, having found a new wakefulness, a renewed interest in life, or maybe just for something else to do, Stew, using his best storytelling voice, relived all his past hunts, every detail of every last one. "I think I've told you about . . ."

"Yes, more than once."

Then Stew told his Little Johnny Jokes, all of which I had heard before, many, many times. Nevertheless, I leaned and listened, nodded and smiled encouragement, and so without my even having to ask he told his Pope Jokes, some of which I had not heard before. When a punch line brought a hesitant half-smile from me and a faintly puzzled look, he would go into a lengthy explanation beginning with, "See, the pope thought . . ." and ending with, "You get it? You get it?" I said I got it. "All right. Good, good." Then he would move on to the next joke and the next, all followed by more puzzled looks and more lengthy explanations and a "You get it?" and again and again I said I got it, even though I never did. You see, it was important to keep these jokes moving, the hours moving, as the moon was moving down the western side of the sky.

The hours passed. The hours piled up. There were still more hours to go as the night wore dumbly on toward dawn. One by one the stars went out and it grew colder. Stew built the fire into a roaring inferno, not just for warmth but to provide the proper atmosphere for the horror stories about to be dragged from their graves. The flickering flames made his face twitch weirdly, gave gaunt, cadaverous shadows to his cheek hollows, and sinister bright points to the skeletal sockets of his eyes. Softly he began to speak. "It was a dark and stormy night . . ."

For an hour he conjured up the stories that had haunted me in my childhood, stories filled with monsters stalking through midnight neighborhoods, trailing seaweed and oozing primordial slime. Just as he was ending the story about the maniac with a hook for a hand, quite without fanfare here came the dawn all pink and red and orange. Here at last came the glorious dawn.

Since that night I have never wanted to go hunting with Stew again. But both of us worry that someday I might.

Van Horn Meadows

September 21: Frozen creek, frozen grasses, frozen tent. The sun is an impotent, formless splotch of light no warmer than a flashlight. Frozen pieces of elk are hanging from every nearby tree. The wind, howling cold from the north, hisses frozen rain against the tent, wherein lies Stew, elk slayer extraordinaire, cocooned inside his mummy, snoring away like some great predatory beast. Beside him I sit swathed in wool from head to toes to fingertips. With Cujo curled warmly, heavily upon my feet I am reading the last inch of *Iron Skillet Bill*. Until the storm lets up or moves out or blows itself out, we can't go home. Our lives are on hold. Not for the first time, not for the last time, I ponder the word "eternal."

Last night we had worked well past midnight preparing the elk for the journey home, Stew always preferring to do this kind of work at night when the flies are denned up. By the light of the campfire, by the light of a waning moon, by the light of a flashlight that would have been lots brighter had I remembered to pack the spare batteries, Stew, with my trained assistance, skinned the elk, separating the hide from the meat with delicate deliberate slices and with all the skill of a brain surgeon. On a blanket of the hide we cut the elk's naked body into pieces small enough to haul home strapped to our backpack frames, nothing over fifty pounds for me, nothing over ninety pounds for Stew. We bagged the pieces–two shoulders, two hams, the pelvis, the neck, and the ribcage cut in two–in old cotton sheets patterned in faded daisies and stitched closed on three sides. If all goes as planned, when the storm lets up we will begin shuttling the meat from this camp to the next camp to the next camp to home, making four trips for every distance covered.

Van Horn Basin

September 23: The sky has cleared finally, but no friendly moon beams down. The forest is an inky, unreal black, black as black gets. We have no campfire jokes tonight, no campfire stories, only the campfire, our aches, our weariness, our hunger, and for our hunger, fried liver. Liver was lunch, liver was dinner, and I told Stew if I ate any more I would get sick. But plead all you want and see where it gets you. I had to eat it, Stew being unsympathetic and liver being perishable (whereas backstrap steaks are not). So I ate it and I got sick, just sort of sick, not bad sick. But I am not just sort of weary. I am bad weary. Nevertheless, I must record these last twelve-odd hours of nonstop pain, the killing effort, the misery, the huge blowing snowstorm. I wish I could blank it all out.

I never saw much of that day. My bifocals were fogged with the steam of my exertion. My back was bent with my cargo of meat bloody and huge, the meaty-end wedged into the small of my back, the foreleg aligned with my spine, the hoof sticking up above my cap. Through the storm, through a screen of white, I stumbled, slid, shot down the clattering talus, trying to match Stew's footprints step for step. My nose ran. My tears froze. My sweat froze. At times I felt I wasn't moving at all but suspended in frozen white space. One time I fell. Tripped up by a tangle of tree roots, my legs couldn't find their right place. I planted myself face-first in the snow, all but crushed by my cargo. My heart stopped. After a few minutes it began beating again, pounding in my ears so it was all I heard. With Stew's helping hand I righted myself, or thought I was righted. For all I knew I could have been upside down.

The trouble with traveling in a wrap-around storm is that you are forced to focus your attention inward. As I zigzagged down from Point A to Point B, I hunkered inside myself and tried to focus on happy end-of-hunt thoughts. Climbing back to Point A, I replayed my past. At Point A, while Stew was saddling me with another piece of meat, I fought off a strong unsettling urge to dive off the cliff into a soaring free-falling half-hideous flight. At Point B, I saw a fleeting image of myself laying prostrate in the snow, hugging Stew's boots, begging him to let me rest, oh please, please, let me go to sleep forever in this nice warm snow.

Cujo and Stew, elk slayer extraordinaire.

I think it was Henry Ford who said, "Whether you think you can or you think you can't – you're right." Stew was chanting this as much for my benefit as for his when dusk descended on that day. We dumped our last load at Point B and camped for the night. We had moved the elk only a mile. What is significant is that we moved the elk at all. We were successful, successful in the sense that neither of us died.

Not too long ago, with the help of our strapping lads, we moved meat homeward twice as fast as we do now. Of course this wasn't the case when the boys were small, their muscles puny, and their enthusiasm was apt to give out halfway from Point A to Point B. Another thing. Back then, we were inexperienced. Although Stew had been trained to his hunting from boyhood, he had not been trained to elk hunting. He didn't know how to pack out something as huge as an elk. This was new to him. He had to learn what worked, what didn't. He learned. We all learned.

Stew was just brimming with ideas. The inspiration for our first portage came from those old black-and-white movies, you know the ones where unclad hunters of tropical rain forests team up in twos and carry poles on their shoulders, poles hung with zebras, gazelles, gnus.

Stew had us team up in twos. He and I took the heavier pieces, Roy and Chad the rest. Here's how it worked. With an elk ham hanging from a pole, a dead aspen sapling, with the smaller end of that pole heave-hoed onto my shoulder, cradled uncomfortably on my shoulder, I would marched double-quick trying to match Stew's mountain man stride, his one foot swinging tremendously in front of the other foot in a way that became quite familiar to me over the next few days. Stew, never one to stop and discuss things, never stopped to discuss things, important things like how we were going to negotiate that maze of fallen timber up ahead, that looming barrier of rocks, that rushing, crashing creek. I had to shout at him just to get him to SLOW DOWN! CHANGE SHOULDERS! TAKE A BREAK!

Meanwhile the boys did their own share of shouting, fighting as only brothers can – I did not! Did too! Did not! . . . Back and forth across their aspen pole they screamed unaffections at each other, and ugly threats. There was a good deal of arguing and boohooing and throwing each other off balance. There was mutiny in their grumblings.

So the following year, to keep things peaceful, Stew came up with another idea, one that improved matters not by much. He hoisted the huge, awkward neck of the elk into Chad's open arms and half of the huge, awkward ribcage into Roy's. Hug them tight, boys.

You're not going to believe what Stew did next. He lashed the boys to their meat, wound round and round them long lengths of thick yellow rope. With a flurry of fingers and twists of his wrists, he tied them up with half hitches, diamond hitches, clove hitches, all those perfect knots only he knew how to untie. And this is the way we moved meat until the boys grew too old to tie up.

It was inevitable that the boys would grow up. It was inevitable that someday they would leave the world of Sawmill Canyon and be on their way to another world, a wacko world, leaving us behind to work out why. They are missed, sorely missed. All that fuss, that loud wonderful fuss. All those small joys that came from being a family. When I pass by our old camps, Stormy Camp, Elk Camp, Deer Camp, I try to force the memories back into the past where they belong, if that isn't being too disloyal to the boys.

How Bear Camp came to be named is a story without a point, or much of a point anyway. But it's a good story, too good a story to go unrecorded. If it seems highly dramatic it is the fault of the story and not the fault of the story teller.

One year I decided the boys should do the camp cooking for a change, I being neither overly maternal nor overly fond of cooking. Since our almost-instant soup was still a few years in the future, someone – and it wasn't going to be me anymore – had to hang around camp all day stirring the simmering beans, adding water to the billycan at appropriate times, and fuel to the fire. Well whenever Roy had the duty, dinner was sort of like a bean paste, warmed over, lumpy, unseasoned. You see, Roy was always on the roam, running down the identity of some mysterious bird. So he was never there to add water or fuel or to even taste anything. Whenever Chad had the duty, dinner was, well, it was somewhat diluted, more like a bean drink than a bean soup, a salty bean drink, so salty it raised blood blisters on our lips. You see, Chad was always hungry and he tasted what he was cooking, tasted it too often, then had to add more water whenever the level in the billycan fell alarmingly low.

Night after night we went to bed hungry and lip-blistered, until Stew, having no other choice, took this mundane domestic matter into his own hands. He decided to stop hunting elk for a while and start hunting deer, something small, something we could finish eating while we were camped, something we could simply cut into chunks, string on willow branches, and barbecue over the dinner fire. Yes, that would work.

It was late the next day when Stew shot the doe, a yearling doe without a fawn. He tagged the carcass, gutted it, skinned it, wrapped it in a sheet, and hung it from the highest limb he could find (the limb wasn't all that high, this country doesn't grow trees all that high).

Meanwhile the sun was sinking. It sank. Stew found himself racing darkness back to base camp, all the while worrying about the meat, would it be safe for the night, just one night. As it turned out, it wasn't. At daybreak we all hiked to the killing site. What a distressing sight. The deer carcass, hanging from a limb too low to accommodate a hanging, had been stripped of its sheet and much of its meat. And there, over there, was a bear, a big old black thing, acting like a campground hooligan, a bear I did not have to bring to anyone's attention.

The bear swiped another jawful of meat, shuffled off a short distance, just five yards or so, and sat on his haunches, unconcerned with our numbers, unconcerned with Stew's murderous stares. The bear started loping around our commotion as if tethered by a rope. He kept this up the whole time we were quartering the carcass and until we carried it off.

Stew had killed this doe on a Sunday, I think it was a Sunday, and the following Tuesday he killed a cow elk early in the morning, so early that by noon he had it ready for transport, that is, it was gutted, skinned, cut into pieces, covered with sheets, and stacked in a pile. The sweaty old sweatshirt he left on top of the pile would protect the meat, maybe,

Mule deer

warn off predators, maybe. For how long? He didn't know.

He rushed back to base camp to round up his packers, all of whom were scattered across the country in three different directions. Hours later than Stew would have liked we all headed out in single file, Stew in the lead, then me, then Roy, then Chad, a tight little procession that soon enough got all strung out. Being in the lead Stew saw it first then I saw it then Roy. It was a little bear working over the pile of elk innards, totally engrossed in the innards, the sponge of lungs, the stinking coil of guts, the steaming mush of semi-digested grass.

Here I must interrupt myself to describe something, if such a thing as Chad's voice can be described, or I should say, these great bursts of voice that preceded him by great distances. Being what it was, this voice had been following us all along, first pleading, then angrily commanding us to wait up. Now this voice came to the little bear. It snapped to attention and turned into a wolverine. Wow!

The wolverine stood atop the gutpile glaring at us, obviously reluctant to leave this monstrous meal, this meal that would feed it forever. After a few minutes it slowly went into the forest, through little patches of light and shade, looking back twice before losing itself in the trees, disappearing for good or perhaps just from our sight, we didn't know and not knowing was of great concern.

Wolverines are so rare in central Idaho you can live your entire life in the bush and never see one even if you were desperately searching for one. While having no personal knowledge of their habits, we had read that they eat everything they can kill, including elk slowed down in heavy snow, and everything they can find, including, we presumed, dead elk left unattended on the ground and dead elk left unattended in a tree, wolverines can climb trees, easily, like cats. According to early nature writer Elliott Coues, what we had here was a "ravenous monster of insatiate voracity, matchless strength and supernatural cunning, a terror to all other beasts."

This wolverine that complicates my story complicated the predicament we found ourselves in as the sun sank in the west. This was the situation. Back at base camp we still had half a deer, entrusted to the gray jays for safekeeping. Here we had this elk, a big elk, a lot of meat to pack to base camp, too much meat to pack in anything less than three or four trips. We couldn't just leave this dead elk unattended, defenseless against that double-hungry wolverine, that ravenous monster of insatiate voracity. What to do. What to do.

What we did still haunts my motherhood, scares me even there. This is not an honorable thing I am about to confess. But after all, Roy begged to spend the night guarding the elk, as if that explains it, explains why we let him, knowing full well his vigil would be lonely, dreadfully long, and if not downright dangerous, then at least vulnerable to danger. Roy was only eleven. He was still a little kid. His unmuscled, kid-scrawny arms were not strong enough to pull Stew's bow, the only weapon we had brought along. In spite of this we said yes, we must have said yes although I don't remember even discussing it with Stew. I know, I know, it sounds crazy to me, too.

In the space of half an hour, Roy brought from base camp everything he thought he would need for the night—sleeping bag, flashlight, a book. Meanwhile Stew and I hoisted the elk, in pieces, into several nearby trees, hung them from the highest limbs we could find, which weren't all that high of course. Roy's campfire had been lit and fanned into an inferno. Long may it burn. With darkness fast approaching, we left him roasting backstraps over serious flames. Surely he would be safe for just one night.

Next morning, having had neither good digestion nor sound sleep, Stew woke us in starlight and we headed out, gnawing on cold leftover liver, stumbling after our flashlight beams, a little worried posse coming to rescue Roy from this wolverine, this terror to all other beasts. Long before Roy's campfire came into view, his piercing unintelligible shouts came into hearing, something that sounded like YAAAH! HAAH! WOOHA! SCRAM! We ran galloping into Roy's camp. What was happening we could not imagine. Was it the wolverine? No. It was the bear.

In what is called an out-of-body experience I saw one of those wild scenes that seem to occur in only our neck of the woods. I am able to see the scene exactly, it so penetrated my mind and effected my dreams. There was the elk ham chewed bare, to the bone. There was the elk shoulder, swinging wildly from the rope. There was the bear, his determination to have that shoulder not nearly as great as Roy's.

Mustering all his courage, all his young mightiness, Roy charged the bear, brandishing a flaming aspen branch in lieu of a real weapon. The bear did not turn himself inside out attempting escape. He simply ambled away, a short ways away, playfully, like some huge, hairy pet Boo Boo. When Roy's weapon burned itself out and he had to return to the campfire to relight, the bear loped back to the meat and swiped another huge chunk. As before, the bear was unconcerned with our numbers, our noise. It was only Chad's cougar scream that drove him off at full throttle. And here by all rights my story should end, with Roy's foolhardy heroics saving our winter meat.

But my story doesn't end here. While Stew was tying the meat to our pack frames I heard this little voice saying (it might have been my little voice), "I hate to say this but the bear is back." And so he was, hunkering down on his haunches, as if for a long wait. Obviously whatever meat we had to leave behind wouldn't be here when we got back. Yet posting another guard was out of the question.

It was left to Stew to do something. He took his bow from its hanging place and stuck in an arrow. On his knees he inched his way toward the bear who was now sticking out his long length of pink tongue and making low menacing sounds, this bear, who at any moment, the next, or the next, might charge. Was Stew scared? Did he even realize the danger he was in? He seemed so utterly alert, so completely unaware of the frantic glances I sent his way. Uh, Stew, tell me what you are going to do. Are you going to shoot the bear? Are you? Do you know how fast a bear can move? How a bear can move faster than you can think, faster than you can shoot? My throat went dry. I had to remind myself to breathe. Yet I felt oddly calm. Why shouldn't I? None of this was really happening. This was only a movie.

What happened next, what I saw, or what I remember seeing, was Stew on his knees, his back bent like his bow. He let loose his arrow. *Thwappp!* Turkey feathers sprouted from the bear's mouth. The bear reacted as he should have reacted all along. His response came as swiftly as a reflex. I blinked my eyes and he was gone. There he was and there he wasn't.

Had Stew not been nervous, had he, with his usual deadeye accuracy – an accuracy born of long practice – struck the bear in the heart, things might have gone differently. We found some blood, not a lot, just a few drops here and there, on a leaf, on a rock, then nothing. We spread out in four different directions, searching for more blood, searching for the bear, everywhere, through every pine grove, behind every boulder pile, in every crease of a canyon. But we found not a trace of the bear, this bear Stew had not wanted to shoot, this poor bear with an arrowhead buried deeply, fatally, in his skull. There you have it. End of story.

Sawmill Creek

September 25: Home sweet home. Our efforts are over. Better yet, the liver is gone. Backstraps for dinner if I want. Days of rest on the couch if I want. I want, I want. I am soused to the gills with fatigue. My meat-hauling muscles are getting too old for this. We need mules.

We need mules or burros or horses or llamas, we haven't decided which, but we'll definitely get something, maybe. Stew and I kick the idea around. Of course, there are plenty of reasons not to get anything at all. Some of these reasons are quite reasonable. They have to do with costs, considerable costs, costs that would exceed our income by a factor of . . . what? two? ten? There are the costs of the beasts themselves, and their shelter, their tack, their feed, their vet visits. There are costs for this, that, and what else we can't imagine, never having been livestock people (we don't even know which end of a horse gets up first). Another good reason not to get anything has to do with the hassle of raising livestock, hassles that would surely complicate our life. So when you really think about it, in retrospect at least, hauling meat our way, the simple way, isn't all that bad, our memories for hardships being quite short. And why get excited about it now. As I see it, from my viewpoint plopped here on the couch, the next elk hunt is very far away, a whole year away. This alone seems reason enough.

8
October

Our village life would stagnate if it were not for the unexplored forests and meadows which surround it. We need the tonic of wildness,–to wade sometimes in marshes where the bittern and the meadow-hen lurk, and hear the booming of the snipe; to smell the whispering sedge where only some wilder and more solitary fowl builds her nest, and the mink crawls with its belly close to the ground
. . . . We can never have enough Nature.
    –Henry David Thoreau

October. Week one. The days cycle quickly from daylight to dark, from rainstorm to snowstorm to clearing. Clouds sweep across the canyon, extinguishing the aspens, igniting them again, each leaf a flame flaring to vivid life. Soon these colors, these screaming colors, will be gone, as if they had never been and could never be again.

There are no mushrooms now, no berries, so my excursions are hollow. My time in the field is hard to put a value on. Nevertheless, I don't feel driven to account for my selfish love of wandering. For any number of trumped-up reasons I walk away from my chores, waft off on a breeze blowing from the heart of the sun. If I must have some pressing duty say it is to witness the autumn ritual of leaves. Some things require my personal presence. Some things I just have to be there for.

"It would do you good to stay home and focus yourself on household matters." Someone might say this. Usually it's a voice inside my head. I don't have to remind myself about the unfinished stories and unanswered letters burning holes in my desk. I should be unpacking the backpacks, sorting through mountains of camping gear, making hills of what has been broken, torn, smashed, bent, what has to be repaired, replaced, thrown out entirely, a total loss. I will get to it, all of it, in due time. I will have time on my hands, too much time on my hands, when the leaves have all dried up and the landscape has turned a dullish leaf-blown brown. Then I will do my chores. Never do I neglect my chores. Never has Stew done them for me. It has never quite come to that.

During nature's downtime I'm a busy woman. On the porch I turn the mummy bags inside out, fluff them back to life. I turn the tent inside out, shake out pine needles, loose matches, a pair of Stew's curled socks, crusty and noxious with fumes. I put porch furniture into storage. I take wool blankets out of storage, air them on the porch. I varnish snowshoes and dust off skis. With a screwdriver poking out my pocket I march importantly along the fence line, cleaning the twelve little houses nailed to the posts, vacant since August. I loosen screws, remove roofs, extract nests, little cups woven with sagebrush, grasses, feathers, and a few bright red threads. From the tree swallow's box I extract quintuplets, their eyes hollowed with decay. What happened here? I check the roof for leaks and find nothing. I check the walls for cracks and find nothing. I find nothing at all that a landlord can fix. Perhaps the Cooper's hawk can account for this.

There isn't much left to do in my rodent-ravaged garden. The plots are just raw earth and wet straw, with a potato or two I have undoubtedly missed. I collect hoses, uncouple their connections, and coil them stiff, crackling with ice. As in traditional households there are certain jobs left to the men, like installing storm windows and cleaning roof gutters, so it will be left to Stew to shut down the water ram for the winter, to drain the dam, the ram, and the underground pipes.

I watch myself puttering around, doing this simple work, this gentle work, this nothing work, while Stew does the real work of tanning the elk hide we brought home. Draping the hide over the fence, flesh side down, hair side up, he pulls out fistfuls of hair until the hide is totally bald. Turning the hide over, bald side down, flesh side up, he scrapes at the little bits of flesh, the clotted webs of blood vessels, the blisters of fat, until the hide is clean, or clean enough anyway. Next he bathes the hide in several solutions: battery acid and water; salt and water; chromium sulfate, salt, and water; baking soda and water; oily soap and water. Then comes the real work I spoke of. Taking the hide off the fence, draping it over a contraption he made (it looks something like the balance beam a gymnast might use), for hours, for days, for over a week, he pulls and stretches and rassles the hide with an effort that bulges his biceps and makes his sinews stand out like guitar strings.

When Stew started tanning elk and deer hides he didn't know diddly about how to do it. Mastering this dying art took a lot of reading, a lot of patience, a lot of determination, and years of getting it wrong before finally getting it right. Sometimes that's just the way it goes around here. I am not as cheerful about this as I sound. I take all Stew's failures for my own, how can I not, they are part of my life too. I give you as an example that contraption he made, not the one that looks like a balance beam, but the one that came before that one, the huge thingy he made out of wood, steel, ropes, and chains, the thingy that was going to take all the pulling-stretching-rassling work out of working the hides. Well it didn't work. It tore the hides is what it did. All that sawing and drilling went for nothing, all that assembling, disassembling, reassembling, puzzling it out, futzing around, giving it another go, for nothing. In the end we had to pay the dump guard ten bucks to get it out of our life.

Another thing Stew tried that didn't work all that well was tanning hides with deer brains like Indian women used to do. Mountain men preferred garments made with this leather, over wool, because it was more durable than wool and softer, having been chewed soft by the Indian women. Personally, I can't see myself chewing on animal skins, and I was massively put out when Stew tried to sucker me into it.

The problem with brain tanning becomes apparent after a few wet-weather outings. Not being waterproof Stew's britches bagged at the knees and in the seat. What is worse they turned stiff and scratchy, like wearing cardboard. This is why he now tans with chromium sulfate instead of brains, even though chromium sulfate is not traditional or aesthetic or even cheap. His britches are still baggy but they are soft come rain or shine.

Tanning with chromium sulfate turns hides gray, a dark gray, about as pleasant a shade of gray as the primer paint of an automobile. So Stew dyes the hides. For boots he uses a commercial black dye that penetrates deeply and stands up to repeated applications of beeswax. For garments he brews his own—onion skins for yellow, carrots for orange, berries for purple, and shaggy-mane mushrooms for black. When he wants a rustier brown than coffee-grounds brown, he steeps iron filings in vinegar. He gets these iron filings for free when he sweeps the floor at Big Jim's Welding.

Stew gets the patterns for his jackets and britches for free, or almost free. When he wants to make a pair of britches, say, he goes to the secondhand store in Challis, and for fifty cents he buys an old pair of jeans. He rips open the seams. He has his patterns.

Much like you would lay out your patterns of tissue paper, Stew lays out his rags, a right leg here, a left leg there, the waistband, pocket, and placket wherever they will fit. He has to follow the grain of the hide. He has to consider the barbed wire scars, the arrow holes, the bullet holes. He has to avoid the elk's belly which is too thin for anything but fringe and the elk's neck which is too thick for anything but boot heels.

Speaking of Stew's boots, they take an entire elk hide to make, an entire winter, too. There are no compromises made, no corners cut, which is why his boots fit like kid gloves and last for years. All fourteen sections of each boot are molded around a right or left last, a foot Stew carved out of wood to match his own. The sections are stitched together by hand with an awl and double-stitched for strength. You can buy boots like these from White's, for hundreds of dollars. Sorry, Stew's boots aren't for sale at any price. He doesn't even have the time or the hides to make me a pair.

Stew is a scrounger, a scraper, a saver of snippets. With leftover leather he made himself a guitar strap, a quiver, a cartridge belt, a shooting vest to cushion the kick of his thunderstick, and a cap to keep his baldness from sun burning. He's a thorough man, Stew. He goes all the way. He even buttons himself up with deer antlers, cut into disks, sanded smooth, and lacquer shined. Tricked out in skins, Buckskin Stew does powerfully capture your attention.

October. Week two. Bam, bam, bam. Bambambambambam. In big-game states like Idaho the opening of hunting season should not be confused with actual hunting. What we have here are recreational hunters. They come roaring into peaceful Sawmill Canyon aboard their nasty snarling ORVs. They come thundering on horses they keep only for this one time of year. From California they come to celebrate their heritage, to share in a social ritual of long standing, and not so incidentally, to win the Big Buck Contest. They shoot their elephant guns at big bucks and big bulls, at coyotes and snowshoe hares, and at the NO HUNTING signs never meant for them. For fear of wandering into their rifle sights, I wander very little now and through the forests not at all. This isn't the case with Stew. He gets into the thick of it with these clowns. We need both an elk and a deer to see us through winter.

Stew steps off the porch, loads his Remington .270, walks across the garden, down the driveway, through the gate, and he is hunting almost at once. From home den to coverts and back to den, like a coyote.Whether his hunt is successful or not, he is always home by sundown or shortly thereafter. Almost always. This one time he wasn't, I got worried, more than worried. Anxiety all but ate me alive.

That night as the clock on the wall ticked away and the hands leaped forward, eight o'clock, eight-thirty, nine, Stew's growing tardiness changed by degrees the atmosphere of the house, turning it slightly sinister. I kept glancing at the clock as if there were some deadline. I kept trying to push anxiety aside. I straightened a rug, picked a thread off the sofa, checked a little stain. I put on music and didn't hear it. I opened the *Messenger* and didn't see the page. One minute I knitted, the next minute I ripped. I moved my feet back and forth across the kitchen, to no purpose, with no intention. For a time I stood quite still and stared out the kitchen window as if by staring I could bring Stew forth from the black night beyond. And the pacing continued in my head.

"Enough of this!" said the little voice in my head. "Get busy, do something." Before Stew returned I would probably have time to do the lunch dishes and set the table. I did the dishes. I set the table. I filled the pepper shaker with pepper and the salt shaker with sugar. I fed the dog, petted the dog, tickled the dog, and shooed him outdoors. I walked myself over to the pantry and cleaned all the shelves (I didn't go so far as to lay down new shelf paper but I thought about it). I filled a bucket with water, soaked my mop, and thumped it to the ground. I swabbed the floor. I stood at the edge, marooned there, watching the water dry in little patches. Nine o'clock, nine-thirty, ten.

With nothing more to keep me from doing so, I went back to the dead-black window and stared out. The tickle of fear in my throat had now grown into a solid lump of something far more complex, far more troubling. This was a terror like the terror of those who stand to lose everything. Could it be that Stew was hopelessly lost? horribly injured? perhaps even . . .

LOCAL HUNTER CAUGHT IN CROSSFIRE, SHOT, KILLED, DEAD.

I tested my reaction to this. As if it already existed, I contemplated my widowhood, the unbearable blackness that would be my life without Stew. Oh, God, don't put me through *that* test. I would be unable to draw another breath. The sun would come up as usual and here I would be at this window unable to move for what is left of my life, or rather my half-life, there would be no one but me, and I am not enough.

Ten o'clock, ten-thirty, eleven. Cujo started barking, his echo bouncing around the canyon. I walked across my spanking-clean kitchen, poked my head out the door, and strained my ears for a sound, any sound. Out from the depths of darkness it came to me like some beautiful music, just these two words, two syllables. "I'm home." Into the lamplight streaming out the kitchen door, Stew emerged, from the dead, grinning with every square inch of his face. I hugged him hard, hard. I wrapped my arms around him, crushed him in relief.

As it turned out Stew had shot a big buck. It had been late and it had gotten dark and he had forgotten his flashlight. So he waited beside a campfire for the moon to rise and light his way home. Simple as that. The deer's heart and liver were in Stew's daypack. Come morning we would roll the rest down in the wheelbarrow.

Stew and I did a lot of talking that night, small talk, nothing talk, while the kitchen's aura of happiness took on by degrees the aroma of sautéed onions. I sat at the table, not helping, just watching Stew as he sliced the liver, taking care to slice it thin, dusting it with flour, browning it, seasoning it, plopping in a can of tomatoes. He took up the whole kitchen and used way more dishes than he needed to and spilled flour on the pantry shelves and trailed flour across the floor and left me with the wreckage. I didn't mind. He could do no wrong. We ate late, leisurely, lavishly, the warm rich goodness made even sweeter by the sugar in the salt shaker.

"Nothing comes easy. Nothing comes free." Stew says this so often we can almost dance to it. By noon the next day, with much gut-busting effort, we had the buck loaded into the belly of the wheelbarrow, tied there with a rope, its three legs folded at the joints, its fourth leg sticking out like a kind of handle. Whether Stew and I and the buck would make it home in one piece was uncertain, almost outside the realm of possibility, the way things were going. Already I was wanting to take back last night's eager offer to help but I couldn't think how to do it.

So here we were, Stew holding the wheelbarrow's handles, and me holding the buck's handle, bumping our load

down from the ridge behind the house, twisting and turning down a slope not merely steep but steep like nowhere
else but here. There were rocks everywhere over which I
was constantly stumbling. The wheelbarrow didn't often
go where we pointed it. To keep it from turning over, at
appropriate times, I was sup-
posed to lift up on my handle,
the sticking-out leg. Lift! Lift!
Don't shove! I am lifting, I am
lifting! But the load turned
over anyway, then a turn or
two later, turned over again.

We bottomed out and lev-
eled off and Stew steered the
wheelbarrow without my help,
rolled it across the creek-worn
canyon floor, across the creek,
across the creek again, under
the aspens, under the firs,
under the cache. Journey's end.

I must explain something
here. There are people in
Stew's meat cache

Challis, I shall not name them, they are found in every
small town, who firmly believe that this cache is a watchtower for our mountain stronghold. You see, it commands
a defensive view of Sawmill Creek, a perfect all-round
view of the enemy's approach, the enemy being the cops,
the Might of Custer County Law. Rumor has it (nudge,
nudge) that we Churchwells grow more than just tomatoes
in our greenhouse. The term "wacky tobacky" passes back
and forth.

Wacky tobacky? Us?

Growing pot is a crime in Custer County on the level
with treason. I don't want the cops to come looking for us
because of something I wrote, not that I'm afraid of cops

mind you, my experience with them has been distant, but exceedingly pleasant. Therefore, I will set the record straight. It is not a watchtower, it is a cache. We don't grow pot in our greenhouse or in our garden or in our crawl-space or anywhere. We don't eat pot in our muffins. We don't smoke it. We don't smoke anything but elk sausage. When I say Stew and I are totally straight, totally square, I'm not being righteous. I have no right to be righteous. You see, drugs are a part of my past, a hangover from my far dark past, albeit with no present meaning.

In the time before Stew, while living in San Francisco, I stuck a flower in my hair and got lost in all that peace and love and LSD of the Sixties. I experimented with all the major drug groups. I don't know why I did drugs, mostly just to see what would happen I guess. When I was twenty I didn't know why I did or did not do anything. My life was a nightclub. It was scary. But I'm not about to go into that now. Already I have shared too much here, gossiped about myself enough. Suffice it to say, I got out alive. Just trust me on this one. It is not a watchtower. It is a cache. This is the whole truth and nothing but.

Bolted to two of the cache's four stilts is a two-by-four draped with a long length of rope. Stew ties one end of this rope to a sturdy branch stuck into slits cut into the hind shanks of these bucks we roll home. Are you with me so far? You might be doing this some day. Anyway with the rope in place we off-load the buck, Stew heaving it upward, hugging the ribs or below the ribs or above the ribs, wherever he can get hold of the slippery sumbitch. Meanwhile I am pulling downward with all my strength on the other end of the rope. Don't, don't, don't let the rope slip! If all goes as planned, and there's no reason it should, the buck will hang from the rope where Stew can skin it handily.

Now that the buck is hideless, headless, and hoofless, it is no longer a buck but a mass of meat to be disjointed, wiped clean with vinegar, bagged in pillow cases, and hung in the cache beside the elk. During October, when days of summer-like weather get the meat sprouting green whiskers of mold, Stew wipes it again with vinegar. By November the meat has frozen hard. It will stay that way until May, or until all that remains of the deer and the elk are the memories of them.

What Stew makes with all this meat is a topic that requires a life of its own, a book of its own, I say this having just finished dinner, having blissfully transferred from plate to fork to mouth a dish Stew calls Heart a la Mountain Man – roast elk heart stuffed with a mixture of bread cubes, elk sausage, and parsnips. Mmm-mmm-good, a dish for the gods.

Stew's excellent cooking requires no assistance from me, and that's good considering I can't do even a simple roast properly. Having no fancy recipes for stir-fries, casseroles, pasta dishes, creamed this, scalloped that, I just chuck in anything at hand and serve with salsa if I'm in a Mexican mood. Being banished from Stew's chaotic kitchen is no more than I deserve.

Cooking is Stew's choosing, his joy, not mine. His cookbook of choice is the *Joy of Cooking*. It can often be found propped up in the only uncluttered corner of the counter, spread open to one greasy page or another: venison burgers, venison meatloaf, venison spaghetti – serious meals, yummy stuff.

Stew has adapted *Joy's* recipe for corned beef into something he calls Corned Beast. This is just your basic deer brisket brined in salt water, cured in the root cellar for three weeks, and simmered until fork-tender. Slice it thinly across the grain. Heap the slices onto a platter with boiled onions, potatoes, and cabbages. Pass the mustard please.

Another recipe from *Joy* Stew likes to fool around with

is headcheese, a sandwich spread made from an elk's head. Alas, this spread lasts for weeks, an elk's head being so huge and all. First off Stew skins the head, soaks it overnight in salt water. Next morning he removes the brine, the slime, the elk blood, the elk hairs, the pine needles, the dirt. He removes those long white thread-like things that look like they could move on their own. With the skull clean, more or less, he boils it until the meat falls off the bones. He grinds everything up, sends it oozing, squishing through the teeth of the meat grinder, everything, the meat, the eyes, the brains, and whatever boiled out of the nose. He pours this muck into loaf pans and chills it. When it's done chilling it looks like a gray lumpy porridge. It doesn't taste all that great but you had better eat it anyway. He went to a lot of work.

When he lived with us, Chad never appreciated Stew's culinary artistry, be it marinated elk tongues, baked marrow bones, fricasseed porcupines, fricasseed flickers, Mushroom Surprise, or Mock Rice Patties. But contrary to what Chad tells anyone who will listen, he was never force-fed. Of course we urged him to open his mind, just take a bite, just one teensy-weensy taste. It was like trying to feed a finicky baby strained spinach, like Chad wasn't old enough to make up his own mind. In fact Chad did make up his own mind. He decided he would not taste any of it, would not like any of it, would be better off not showing up for meals at all.

Now imagine if you will a Kansas kitchen, another chaotic kitchen. Standing at the counter with her *Joy* propped open, Grandma Churchwell is stirring something chocolately or caramelly or marshmallowy, some kind of healthy sweet. Chad is sitting at the kitchen table robotically feeding his face with Gummy Worms or Goldfish or Dizzy Grizzlies or Screaming Yellow Zonkers, taking large gobbling bites, licking his fingers. And all the while he is eating these things, he is complaining to Grandma about all the weird stuff his folks made him eat. "Even *flowers*."

"Is there anything they don't eat?"

"Yes. Hooves. They don't eat hooves."

Stew slaves over these meals for nobody's benefit but his own. He has the appetite for the exotic, the weird, not me. Myself, I like food. Period. Food is what I get out of bed for in the morning. Food is what I come in for when it's cold. Unfortunately, I never know what I might be eating for the first time in my life, Stew's culinary imagination being what it is. But rattlesnakes? Come on. Gimme a break!

I had thought this was going to be a perfectly normal trip to town. And it was, until we drove home and Stew spotted this rattlesnake, a brawny heavily-built rattlesnake, sunning its very long length in the middle of Morgan Creek Road. And guess what he wanted to do with this rattlesnake. He wanted to try it fried. "Sure," I said when Stew asked me if I was game. I have resigned myself to Stew's eagerness for experimenting with Sawmill Creek cuisine. I have resigned myself to the fact that I am married to a man whose standards of what's normal have been seriously eroded. Besides, had I said no, Stew would have taken no notice.

You can't casually walk up to a rattlesnake, pick it up in your hands, wring its neck, and take it home. You have to approach it with a cautious confidence, and a long-handled shovel. Having approached this snake cautiously, if somewhat unconfidently, Stew waved the gleaming end of his short-handled shovel over the snake, testing its reaction. It reacted. It reacted so quickly it defied belief. Its body tensed, slitted pupils shifted, forked tongue flicked out and in, tasting the air, sizing up the situation, sizing up its size against the size of the shovel. With lidless yellow eyes it stared at the shovel, at its own death, and made ready its fearsome fangs.

Assuming a little less confidence, Stew raised the shovel high over the snake's head and brought it smashing down, missing the snake by a few inches. Up jumped the snake's head. It drew back as if to strike, did strike, the shovel. I heard the click of fangs against the steel. I saw the stain of venom, a witches' brew of enzymes capable of digesting human tissue. Out flicked the tongue again. Up went the head, weaving higher and higher, as high as it would go, until it toppled over. The rest was mercifully brief. Having sized itself against the size of Stew, the snake straightened itself explosively, strung itself out long and vulnerable, and made off for the bushes. In rushed the shovel, pasting the snake's head to the road, chopping it off for good measure. The snake was dead.

Stew wanted to eviscerate the snake at home on the kitchen counter where it was convenient. And he did that, or he tried to do that. But when he poked the steely point of his knife into the snake's scaly belly, four feet of dead snake shivered and this shiver went back through the knife, up Stew's arm, down his spine, and into his very guts. Apparently this snake was not quite dead. Stew clamped his bearded jaws in determination. Assuming a little more dignity than was necessary, his focus unblinking, he poked the snake's belly again. Again the snake shivered. Stew's unshakable composure was so badly shaken he postponed evisceration until morning. "This must be why," I wrote my mother, "not too many people eat snakes."

The morning was a long time coming. All night I drifted in and out of consciousness, unable to make my mind entertain any other image but the snake corralled in the kitchen sink, scraping its scales against the stainless steel. I couldn't bear to hear it and I couldn't hear anything else. I kept the covers pulled over my head even though it was too warm. Beside me, someone was moaning, whimpering, pillow wrestling.

Not until the wee hours did the snake make its last twitch. Was it really, finally, forever dead? Would it stay dead? No! It was slithering across the rug, with ten more snakes. I screamed and screamed but no sound came out of my mouth.

Slowly I came awake. Somehow it was morning, the terrible night was over. I smelled something cooking, sizzling in butter. Snake steaks. "They tasted wonderful," I wrote my mother, "more than wonderful, and I never want to eat them again. I'm glad I tried them but once is enough. Know what I mean? You can really overdo this kind of thing."

October. Week four. Abruptly, overnight, the hunters are gone. The guns are stilled. The silence in Sawmill Canyon is total, eerie, like a city after the BOMB. There is only the will of the wind, the sound of the wind in the aspens, rattling the bark hanging like shreds of torn wallpaper, stripping the branches bare, to a leaf, silencing their restless quaking. The wind blows leaves into the air, herds them noisily across the hard-frozen ground, the frozen summer grass, and into the creek running black beneath a thin skim of ice. This wind so full of winter empties out the land, runs the bears into their dens and the chipmunks into our woodpile. The birds, all my lovely birds, are fueling up at the feeder and flying south, flying off to become someone else's birds. Mornings and evenings, with a mixture of sorrow and delight, I watch snow geese go honking by, streaming by like strands of pearls, so high in the sky their white underbellies flash back the sun riding low on the ridges, the ridges ragged with evergreens cut black against the skyline. Soon the wild herds, having congregated with a sudden purpose, will leave for lands of lesser snows. All winter they will line the highway like hitchhikers at a freeway onramp.

I need to acclimate myself to this meanest of seasons, this non-season, this absence of life. I shiver in the wind. Now nature is no comfort against the oncoming loneliness, this loneliness already gathering around me. Nevertheless, my great love for wandering gets the better of me, a love I can never get my fill of. I leave Stew in a pile of sawdust, in a pile of logs it is my chore to haul to the woodbox. Something unclear calls me to the forests, to the well-trodden paths I have walked alone a hundred times before. If I keep walking straight ahead, in my present mood, I could make the mouth of Morgan Creek before dark. Thumb a lift to Challis Airport. Fly to Idaho Falls. Change planes. Fly to Salt Lake City, Las Vegas, Palm Springs. Call Mom. Surprise! Here I am.

My homing instinct turns me around, toward home. As I walk under the bare-limbed aspens, I realize I am not tragically alone here, there is no reason to feel, as I do nevertheless feel, so achingly lonely. I have Stew, and he is, just barely, enough.

9
November

Every man looks at his wood-pile with a kind of affection.
    –Henry David Thoreau

Hauling wood is a less than delightful activity. We do it in springtime so as not to cut short our summer's recreation (it's important to keep priorities straight here). Consequently, by November we have ten cords standing out back in what can only loosely, very loosely, be defined as a stack. There are ten rows, head high, wide at the bottom and tapered at the top, sometimes stable, more often not. That is to say, I am the wood stacker and I do the best I can.

This should be enough wood to see us through winter. Should be. We have no way of knowing. The winter might be mild, and by mild I mean that temperatures drop no lower than the minus twenties and for just a few weeks at that. Then again the winter might be unreasonable, severe, and by severe I mean like on the moon, the dark side, in the off season. If we ever ran out of wood while we are snowbound I don't know what we would do. That kind of crisis, why take chances. So in November we go for the one last load we dare not do without.

Dust gusts around us, spins beneath the wheels. Branches pop beneath the wheels as the truck labors along in four-wheel-drive, rattling over cattle guards, splashing across creeks, bouncing over the dens of sleeping rodents, bouncing out of one rut and into another. We take some lefts, some rights, some dead-ends. Around one bend and we are looking down over the trees, around another bend and the trees are looking down on us.

These old logging roads go nowhere. They simply stop, cease to exist, somewhere back there. Stew backs the truck down and around and around to where we passed acres of skinny trees crisscrossing the forest floor. This is the site of what the Forest Service calls a "sanitation cut." The public is welcome to clean up this mess, for five bucks a cord.

With a measuring tape and marking pen Stew sections a tree into lengths that will fit into our stoves. With his chainsaw he buzzes the tree apart. He raises the logs mightily over his head and heaves them down the hill. They roll and roll and roll and come to rest in several piles, against a fence post, against a tree stump, against a boulder. Here's where I come in. With a kick I roll-start the logs, roll them on down to their final resting place beside the truck, or if my kick is too hard, too askew, they come to rest beyond the truck, way the heck down there beside the creek. I jot down their location in my head, hoping some idea of how to get them back up will come along. This is not very efficient, I know. Call it inefficient. Yes, use that word. I'm not sensitive. I won't get excited. After all, when has efficiency ever had anything to do with anything I do, even for a minute.

The logs pile up. The hours go by. I load ten logs onto the tailgate of the truck. I load myself onto the tailgate. I crawl under the camper shell. I stack the logs in a row at the back. I jump down from the tailgate. I load ten more logs. The logs are heavy. There are lots of logs.

Stew and I keep pace with each other, or we don't, it doesn't matter, we're on mountain time which is no time at all. It wasn't always like this. Back when Stew tried to fill some stupid self-assigned quota, bossing himself around, a little of the slave-driver in his own driven soul, he would go whizzing through the forest, his mouth made into a little determined line, his chainsaw screaming, the chain of teeth whirring, these teeth sharper than shark's teeth, eager to dismember a tree or a tree-cutter, makes no difference which. Stew had been heading for trouble and it came one day. Carelessly he let the saw brush against his thigh before giving the chain enough time to wind down to a stop. Before his reflexes kicked in, the saw chewed open his tough elkskin leggings and his soft manskin underneath. The damage never went beyond bandages but this wasn't the case with a guy we know, another backyard woodcutter, who all but cut off his hand and did cut off three fingers, the horrid details of which I will leave to your imagination.

Having tested his luck enough, Stew decided to slow down, to cut half a cord instead of a full cord each trip. There were no objections from me.

We conserve wood in winter – as we should have done all along – by wrapping ourselves in wool and keeping the house several degrees below toasty. On crackling bitter nights we pile on wool blankets and take Cujo to bed to keep our feet warm. We cut our living space in half by closing off the north side of the house – the bathroom and our offices. We move our desks into the living room, well within the warming range of the stove. For six months we share this cozy space although this stresses our marriage. You see, above the clattering of Stew's ancient Underwood there are a pair of ears quite handy for critiquing my work. And above the clattering of my ancient Royal there are another pair of ears just as handy for critiquing his work. "So do you want me to tell you it's fine? or do you want my opinion?" In order to get back to one's work, this generally amounts to the same thing.

We conserve our wood supply but not our food supply. We stockpile food in quantities to feed the proverbial army, so much food, as if we were expecting a siege – fresh meat, dried sausage, jerky, fresh vegetables, dried vegetables, dried mushrooms, dried berries. You would think this would be enough to last a winter. It is not. However much we want to, we can't survive on what we produce by hunting, gardening, and foraging. We have to buy white man's food.

We buy food and most of our supplies only one time a year, nonbrand items in bulk quantities, in economic sizes, in cardboard boxes and plain brown sacks with simple labels: Rolled Oats. Short-grain Rice. Wholewheat Flour. Ordering this much food just once a year runs my life the first week in November.

I can't just guess at what we will need, I have to know what we will need, and I do know, pretty much, with the help of a simple system I have devised. Here's how it works. When I open a sack of oats, for example, I take a felt-tip pen and record the date right on the sack. When the last cup of oats is scooped out of the sack, I record that date too. After subtracting the second date from the first date I see that Stew and I breakfast for six months on one fifty-pound sack of oats, that's two sacks a year. I do this with everything: sacks of beans, sacks of barley, cases of coffee, cases of syrup, cases of canned tomatoes, everything. And always, faithfully, I record the results on my chart. So when it comes time to order I take chart in hand and order for the whole year accordingly.

This system, such as it is, always needs fine tuning from year-to-year, not so much nowadays as in the past, when the boys were little, then bigger, then big, then gone. One year, Stew's dietary caprices messed me up. In February he decided one morning, just like that, to stop putting milk on his oatmeal. He had read that dairy products are unhealthy. That same February, by some reasoning that defies easy understanding, he started using twice the amount of margarine I allotted him on my chart (partially hydrogenated soybean oil, diglycerides, emulsifiers, and sodium benzoate don't seem altogether healthy). As a result we had too much of this and too little of that.

One winter we ran out of dog food. It wasn't so much that Stew . . . but hold on, this takes some telling.

To begin with I should explain that in the years gone by, thankfully gone by, we always got a hog to eat in exchange for mucking out hog pens, or rather Stew and the boys mucked out the pens, I buried their clothes afterwards. For reasons too complicated to detain us here, Stew hauled these hogs home, alive, in the bed of the pickup (the pickup was enclosed with a stock rack he built for reasons having nothing to do with hauling hogs). Well the year we ran out of dog food was a good year for the hog market. The rancher sold most of his hogs. So he gave Stew the choice between a little pink piglet and a thousand-pound boar, a barge of a boar, enough sausage to feed us for a lifetime.

Stew lowered the tailgate of the pickup. He put the ramp in place. Rope in hand, he went for the big guy. The boar roared, pawed the ground, blew flames out his snout. Stew stopped to reconsider. He did reconsider. He went for the piglet.

"What the heck," said the rancher. "I shorted you on meat this year, take this here puppy. Purebred German shepherd." Sure! Uh huh! Believe that and you'll believe anything. Not only was this pup a mutt, he was the last of the litter, the one nobody wanted even for free, nobody that is but Stew. Begging Cujo's pardon, I sure didn't want him. For foolish reasons I have always wanted in the worse way one of those foolish bug-eyed mini dogs, a little snuggle of joy with maybe a pompom at the end of her tail. Muffin I'd call her.

At any rate, home we went, squealing piglet in back, and in front, hiding under my legs, the furry ball of trembling fear we misnamed Cujo, after Stephen King's canine killer. We still had Oggy back then, so we fed Cujo the same kibbles Oggy ate, only much less, he was so small. When I was getting ready to order I simply added together what each dog ate in a month, multiplied by whatever, then added an extra fifty-pound sack for Cujo to grow on. One extra sack. Just one. That was in November. By March Cujo's appetite was way bigger than it should have been. Cujo was way bigger than he should have been, not bigger than a pony perhaps, but not smaller either. Here's how big he was. He was nose-high to the dinner table and the dinner table was where his nose was apt to be found at dinner (he didn't care where he put his big feet).

By April we were almost out of dog food. Then we were. The dogs ate bread until we ran out of flour. The dogs ate pork until we ran out of piglet. Finally it became a matter of whoever got to the table first and ate the fastest got fed.

Now that Oggy is gone and Cujo has grown all he is going to, or I should say, all he is going to get to, I still double-order dog food, along with anything else we wouldn't want to winter without (winter brings enough hardships as it is). Before mailing my order to the market I check it, check it again. How many times, how many times? I tick off each item in my head while I am up to my elbows in soapsuds: detergent, sponges, pot scrubbers . . . while I am up to my elbows in bread dough: flour, bran, yeast . . . while I am waiting for sleep: lentils, split peas, black-eyed peas, pintos, kidneys, whites, great northerns, baby limas . . . zzzzzz. Beans are so boring.

Three, four, or five weeks later we pick up our order. Main Street is humming with enterprise, with festivity and friendliness, with sounds of people in happy transactions. The owner of Lamb's Market greets us with a hardy

welcome, just short of a bear hug, although he hardly
knows us. It isn't so much that he is overly friendly as he
is damn glad we have finally come to pick up our order
piled high on pallets, pallets his clerks have had to walk
around, work around for weeks.

Aboard a dolly our plunder rolls out the stockroom to
the loading dock, where Stew stacks the sacks and boxes
in the bed of the pickup and I check everything off my list.
Beans. Check. Rice. Check. Oats. Check. Flour, wheat, popcorn, salt, dried milk, sugar, pancake syrup, jelly, peanut
butter, mayonnaise, mustard, vinegar, vegetable oil,
canned tomatoes, coffee, margarine, toilet paper, matches,
dish washing soap, bleach, storage bags, dog food . . .
Check-check-check.

The pickup is so loaded down in back it rises in front,
rises so high we see more of the sky than the highway
home. With the back bumper bumping every bump in the
driveway, Stew backs up to the storage shed. I unload. He
stacks. What a sense of replenishment, of security, of well-
being, even though some shelves remain empty, reserved
for our last trip to town.

Over the aisles of the generic brands area, banners celebrate Mrs. Whosit's new line of stuffing mixes. Here Stew
and I linger, talking to a few friends and making a few ran-
dom selections from the shelves: yeast, baking soda, dental floss, paper towels, garbage bags, razor blades . . . Some
of these items we don't use in large enough quantities to
order in bulk. And some of these items just somehow got
left off my list.

Across town, at the propane plant, we fill ten five-gallon bottles with enough gas to light our long winter nights.
And since these gaslit hours need to be filled somehow
without the benefit of television or friends, we stop by the
Challis Library and weed through their shelves of give-
aways, their stacks of romance novels, westerns, myster-

ies, sci-fi, there isn't much else. If only the library had a lending program for the snowbound. If only our budget was a little bigger, big enough to buy a winter's worth of books, good books. If only . . . but that will do. With sighs heard round the world we load up on books we have no interest in reading.

Up Main Street from the library, two minutes, is the Hub, the throbbing-heart essence of the Challis community. The Hub is staffed by volunteers from the community. Its annual income, thousands of dollars, goes back to the community via Search and Rescue, the EMTs, the library, the historical society, the arts council, the fireworks fund, the scholarship fund.

For those of us not prey to fashion, the Hub is a department store. For a dime, a quarter, a few bucks you can get second-hand and third-hand dresses, slacks, shoes, socks, tee shirts in colors, and tee shirts in white (well, whitish). Bargains like these bring bliss to my eyes. We hike, we sleep, we shop – we raised the boys – in hand-me-downs. It doesn't matter that emblazoned across my chest are messages not of my choosing. DIE, YUPPIE SCUM. I flaunt foot races I haven't run, concerts I haven't seen, and floods I haven't survived.

Next stop, the Suds 'n Spin, where we stuff a dozen washing machines with dirty laundry, we have lots of laundry, never have I seen anyone with this much. Of course, no one lives like we do, does laundry like we do. Our sheets, blankets, and towels won't see another soak-slosh-spin cycle until spring.

While the dryers click and toss our laundry around we finish our rounds in town. We stop at the Village Inn and for a dollar or two pick up the five-gallon plastic pickle buckets that will see a second life as clothes-washing-rinsing buckets. We stop at the American Legion Hall (our last trip to town always coincides with the general election), where we cancel out two votes of the Wise Use Movement. Last stop, the Copper Kettle Cafe for chocolate shakes. This is our idea of eating out and this is the only time we do it. Even so, when we blow a few bucks like this I have to close my eyes, miser that I am with our budget.

Having loaded the pickup with every conceivable thing we will need to insure our winter well-being, having nothing left to do, nowhere else to go, we leave Challis's cheerful neighborhoods and return to our lonely distant own. During the winter, during the next six months of social sterility, Stew and I will come to realize that we are social creatures after all, at least around our edges.

The last week in November, traditionally, and even in our time here on Sawmill Creek, the fickled gods of snowstorms begin their serious work even as we are finishing ours. Stew winterizes the truck, that is to say, he checks the antifreeze, changes it if he has to. He parks the truck in the driveway in such a manner it can be roll-started in May if it won't start any other way. Finally, he removes the battery and stores it in the root cellar where it won't freeze even when temperatures fall to their bottomless depths.

We will spend no more money until May, not even for Christmas, especially not for Christmas. So I tally my accounts down to the last penny, put my books in apple-pie order. There is never a discrepancy between my books and reality. I submit the following not for verification, like an audit, but more like a certificate of honor. I submit it exactly, with cents rounded off and a few clarifications added.

Expenses 1994

Food and Supplies $362
Clothing $16
Propane (for lights and a one-burner stove) $52
Hunting and Fishing Fees $82

Firewood Cutting Fee $50
Property Tax $391
Vehicle Registration Renewal $25
Vehicle Liability Insurance (required by law) $128
Gasoline (estimated) $300
Truck Maintenance $584
Medical (to irrigate my plugged up ears) $37
Dental (my teeth are dying two at a time) $30
Veterinary (worm medicine and flea collar) $36
Backpacking Supplies (Stew's new backpack) $104
Archery Supplies (feathers and arrowheads) $30
Reloading Supplies (bullets) $28
Miscellaneous Expenses $100

Total Expenses $2,355

With the right mate, and I have this, being cramped by poverty can be a game, not a fun game exactly, it's way too complex and perplexing to be that. There is inflation to deal with, to plan for, to prepare for. There are rises in postal rates and sales tax rates even as interest rates on our savings accounts continue to fall. Our property tax can increase with a decrease in the tax base or with an increase in county expenditures or with an increase in the assessed value of our place. Propane prices and gasoline prices can increase with a decrease in supply and an increase in demand. Hunting fees and fishing fees and fees for collecting firewood can increase and do increase at the whim of agency managers.

But these expenses have never increased, even insignificantly, all in one year. In fact some expenses like clothing, vehicle registration, and vehicle liability insurance haven't increased in a decade. That's good because some expenses have increased wildly and will continue to do so, can be expected to do so, so much is beyond my fiscal control. Mainly I worry about meeting future medical expenses, as well I might at my age, with Social Security benefits still a decade away and insurance premiums way beyond our budget. Living without medical insurance means living with a foolish faith, an unfounded expectation, that fortune will continue to smile on Sawmill Creek. Living without medical insurance means having to juggle the rest of the household accounts when adversity eventually strikes. A few summers ago I had to do just that.

The trouble began where trouble usually begins, right from the start. Before the third strange thing happened to me, there had been the first.

One afternoon in early summer I stepped off the porch in the very same manner I have stepped off the porch a million times before (something nowhere as ambitious as leaping from the railing). With a sudden thud I was no longer standing but sprawled on the ground. Through a fog of blinding pain, I yelled out the details to Stew: Porch. Fell. Ankle. It hurt more than it should have. It was swelling and bruising grotesquely. This kind of thing called for x-rays, the bill for which is the point to this. Paying the bill not only wiped out the funds set aside for Medical, but the funds set aside for Dental as well. This would have been no problem if the second strange thing had not happened to me.

It was now midsummer and five baby barn swallows were huddled under the porch roof, white-washing everything. I was on my hands and knees scrubbing away when something–to call it a splinter would understate it significantly, to call it a stick would not be farfetched – got jammed beneath my fingernail. It was so deeply and painfully embedded, it had to be removed professionally under local anesthetic ($$$). Well having already bankrupted two of my accounts I now did so with a third, my

Recreation Account, which in effect canceled our fall trip to Yellowstone.

Then in late summer the third strange thing happened to me. Leaving the lunch dishes in the sink I had gone out to the porch to watch the approach of a boisterous storm, watching boisterous storms being my kind of fun. Scooting my willow chair to a protected pocket of the porch, I sat and listened to the tempest of wind and thunder. In the space of a minute I counted two dozen lightning strikes, cloud to cloud, cloud to ground, never less than two dozen, often more. Van Horn Peak was smoking as pine trees, one after another, burst into flames, only to be extinguished by curtains of rain, great sheets of rain slanting eastward, coming up the canyon. Rain hit the tin roof with the sound of fat frying, and still I did not go into the house until I was thrillingly drenched. The rain forced its way in behind me.

By now my eyes were red and crying profusely. They felt scratchy, full of sand. When my discomfort worsened Stew drove me though the storm to the clinic in Challis. After an examination and some extensive questioning, the doctor said my injury was caused by lightning. The flash burns I suffered were much like the flash burns welders suffer when they foolishly work without a protective hood. My injury was temporary, easily treated at home with bed rest and aspirin. That was good. But I still had this exam to pay for and that was bad. I had to bankrupt another account, an account that will go unnamed. I don't want the game cops to come looking for Stew. I'm kidding! I'm kidding!

So there you have it. That's just the way some summers go. Or they go like this:

Let me begin by saying that it is not in vain I have been given the gift for fiscal wizardry, as it is not in vain Stew has been given the knack for automotive repair.

Although our truck has seen more miles than the space shuttle, he keeps it running, and reliably so, with a program of preventive maintenance and with funds set aside for brake jobs, lube jobs, rebuilding the front end, the rear end, the transmission. Generally, Stew's program causes me no financial problems. Generally. Not always. The summer he rebuilt the engine was an exception. The cost of parts and the cost of machine work built up to a nightmare of expense, and Stew spent rather more money than I had set aside in Truck Maintenance. I had to come up with more money. Quick. No time for anything elaborate.

I got an idea, an idea that didn't involve juggling accounts, a crazy idea that came to me in the idiocy of sleep. I can't imagine why I had to bully Stew into it but I did. So there we were rooting around in the cobwebby corners of the loft, sorting through boxes of old journals, photo albums, dusty catalogs, magazines, boxes of things Stew had crated home from the Hub, from auctions and yard sales, things of questionable value, things that were chipped, twisted, cracked, and sprung, most of them missing their vital parts. Where I am a firm believer in throwing it away until it hurts, Stew can't bear to throw anything away. Once bought by Stew Churchwell they are his forever. Is that an apple press? Is that a bottle capper? Is that a . . . what is that anyway?

All these things were dusted off, fixed or not fixed, and arranged in some order on old blankets spread across the meadowy mouth of Sawmill Creek. Empty cardboard boxes weighed down with rocks stood in wide spots on Morgan Creek Road, announcing our yard sale in big black letters, a yard sale, by the way, unsanctioned by the Challis National Forest, unbeknownst to the Challis National Forest. Nobody knew about this event, nobody but the whole town.

Everybody came, separately or together in caravans,

with picnic lunches and with lots of lovely money. The dollars flew at us so fast we couldn't keep them sorted. We just stuffed them in our pockets and only counted them at the end. We were agog. Our cup of joy fairly overflowed. Not only was there money to finish fixing the truck, having managed to inch past the break-even point, we bought two factory-fresh mountain bikes, his 'n' hers.

Well that's about it so far, no real crises, no creeping lava of financial disaster. But as you can see, our life, like every life, has its troubles. Our theme is only one in a thousand variations. But what worries me – and I take no joy in breaking the news to you – is this: If we are to continue living here in perpetuity, as we have planned, if we are to continue living this life we have dreamed about, this life we have grown accustomed to, then we must continue living within our budget (the loft is all but empty). We cannot afford to drain off the principal of our investments. My job as I see it, my plain and not-so-simple job, is to make sure we don't ever have to work for wages again. Excuse me now. I'm in a bit of a hurry. I have to figure out how to pay for Stew's new reading glasses. Don't worry. Some idea will come along.

10
Winter

*We must learn to reawaken and keep ourselves
awake, not by mechanical aids, but by an infinite
expectation of the dawn, which does not forsake us
in our soundest sleep.*
–Henry David Thoreau

The mornings of December, long before sunrise, coyotes give us a wake-up call. Sleeping late is Stew's idea of sin, so it is he who must go forth into the cold dark house, while I stay under the covers until the last possible moment. Slowly, with much yawning and stretching of limbs, Stew gets out of bed and lights the lamps. He crumples up a few pages of the *Messenger* and arranges them on top of the cold ashes in the Earth Stove. Painstakingly he constructs a nest of twigs and sticks, arranging every-thing methodically, symmetrically, overly neat. On top of this nest he balances four small logs. He scratches a match. We have Fire.

The chimney chuffs smoke. The tea kettle whistles. Buried to our chins in puffy quilts and wool knits, we read our books and drink our first mugs of coffee, then our sec-ond, then several more, me in my jammies, Stew in his jolly red union suit. Through the windows we watch for the coming of the dawn. And the dawn does not forsake us.

This far north, the winter sun rises reluctantly, long past ten o'clock. When the sky is snowy or overcast, sun-rise is but a smear of light, nothing more. Ah, but when the sky is unclouded, the air stunningly cold, sunrise is incredible. Who could ever tire of this scene at the windows, the way the moon sets pale and delicate as porcelain in a rosy wash of sky, the way Van Horn Peak comes on all pink and glowing. When the sun shoots over the eastern ridge, presto! Sawmill Canyon explodes with ice crystals. Crystals catch the sun and flash it back in rainbow points. Crystals describe the aspens, every branch, every twig, and the firs, every needle, every cone. Even the air fizzes with crystals. When nature goes mad what a world!

Slippers slapping across the floor, I go exploring from window to window. Looking through the southern window, frosted with ice inside, a thin, flaky, delicate coating, looking through my own reflection, I see the snow laying white and perfect, all the more lovely since we don't have to shovel it. I see the drifts banking against the bushes, making dunes of the bushes, and the fence tops poking through, everything so familiar, so dear. I see the old coyote the boys named Wiley. After all these years he's still here. Binoculars affixed to my face I watch him pounce on a mouse, trying to wrest a meal from the harsh morning. He misses the mouse. He always misses the mouse. He lifts his leg on the far fence post, leaving behind a lemon snowcone. He makes his way on down the creek, trotting, stopping, listening, crossing the creek, hot on the scent of something, now off the scent, now on again, finding, losing, wanting whatever it was, probably a snowshoe hare, camouflaged, white on white.

Speaking of snowshoe hares, there are usually a few sharing the woodpile with the chipmunks, protected there from the likes of Wiley and his kin. They eat the rose bushes growing in thorny thickets beside Stew's shed. Through the spotting scope aimed out the kitchen window I watch rose branches, thorns and all, disappear between magnified bunny lips.

Van Horn Peak looms above our cabin.

Through the living room window, my big proprietary window, I watch my chickadees, three tough little fluffs I love in my simple-minded way. Upon finding me at my desk they give me this look to say they are running low on peanut butter.

Roy built this bird feeder years ago, for my winter amusement. It is the be-all and end-all of bird feeders. It has a pitched roof that shelters the seed tray, and the seed-eating birds. It has a metal cone on the post that prevents the passage of seed-eating mice, my love for mice being utterly dormant.

At each end of the tray a large wire cage holds slabs of elk suet. There are perching pegs just below, rather small-ish pegs that discourage the perching of big birds like magpies and crows, birds I love even less than mice. Gray jays perch easily on the pegs. Whistling softly, they chip-chip-chip at the fat. Clark's nutcrackers perch not as easi-ly on the pegs. Unlike the gently jays, they are boisterous and noisy as crows. With their big bills they bully away the jays and attack the fat with the force of jackhammers, their grating nasal *kra-a-a-a-a* bursting out in white puffs of frozen bird breath. In turn the nutcrackers are bullied away by the bird with the biggest bill of all, a male flicker, same bird every year–black bib, spotted shirt-front, lapels lined in orange, face smeared with red lipstick–yep, same bird, same clown who forgoes the fall migration for these easy meals, this never-ending feast of fat.

I watch windows like I used to watch TV. At window number four Cujo appears, dancing on legs balled with ice. Above Cujo, Stew appears, his beard frosted with ice, his mustache dripping needles of ice, his cheeks rosy with cold and the exertion of before-breakfast chores. Through the window Stew greets me with the exuberant superiority of an outdoor person greeting a sedentary friend. Ax in hand, he asks if I need cookstove wood today, meaning, will I bake bread today. Only if it's too cold to ski.

These winter mornings there isn't much we do you'd call work, in the sense that ranch-bound ruralites have work that gets them out of bed and into the cruel uncaring dawn to attend to the demands of their livestock, to feed the cows, to feed the horses and pigs and chickens, the whole morning, feeding something. There isn't much we do you'd call work in the sense that desk-bound urbanites have work that gets them rushing out of bed, into the shower, into their nice clothes, slamming house doors, slamming car doors, streaming en masse to attend to the demands of their bosses. Stew and I are never going anywhere during the morning rush hour except to the stove for more coffee.

But we can't laze around all day. We do have a few chores. Every morning Stew loads the box on the porch with firewood for the Earth Stove, and on my bread-baking days he loads the box beside the cookstove. Every morning he chops out the ice covering Sawmill Creek and fills two five-gallon pickle buckets with enough water for coffee, cooking, washing dishes, and such. He fills two more buckets if it's Monday, our day to wash clothes, or if it's Saturday, our day to take baths. If the pantry is low on food he fetches more food from the shed. If the fridge out back is low on meat he fetches an elk or deer quarter from the cache (it will be defrosted, carved into roasts, hamburgers, and stews, then packaged in butcher paper). If it's a slow day Stew's chores end with breakfast.

Here's what I do. First off I pop Bach into the tape player since I do my best work to music. I do the breakfast dishes and make the bed. For me that's a good day's work. Once in a while if I feel like it I dust along the mantels, using the open palm of my hand, or I blow dust bunnies around on the breeze of my broom. I don't like doing housecleaning, housekeeping, house taking care of, but I like having done it. I feel better when I have done it and I feel better about myself.

It isn't my mother's fault that my house is not a paradise of cleanliness. All the summers I was growing up, when there wasn't much else to do, she taught me how to do this domestic stuff. This is how you make the bed; this is how you load the dishwasher; this is how you vacuum the mantel; this is how you vacuum the rug; this is what you do if guests are coming; always check the temperature of the room; always check the freshness of the air; always check the tablecloth for stains, the napkins for stains, the glasses for spots; this is how you set the table; forks go to the left except the very small fish forks that go to the right; spoons, including the iced-tea spoons, go to the right; knives go to the right, sharp edges toward the plates. My mother taught me all right. I just didn't get it.

Since I have not been given the gift of domesticity, my house is not always clean. But my house is always neat, a model of organization. I cannot break my lifelong habit of wanting things put back where they belong, where I can find them again. Stew doesn't get it. He confuses clutter with a homey lived-in look. He has been petrified into his flyblown bachelor ways. Anyway, this is what I think when I peek into his office, his domain, the perfect mess.

I am not allowed inside his workshed either, his guy's place, but occasionally I peek in there too. I peer through the grubby gloom, through the rolling clouds of dust rising sluggishly from the floor. Behold that calendar from the Sierra Club, three years old and still hanging on the wall beside the black outlines for the tools he keeps on his workbench, piled there with piles of projects unfinished, abandoned when the interest gave out, and stacks of fix-it manuals leaning over in apparent defiance of gravity. Look upon the coffee cups, cobwebs spun across the top, dregs at the bottom, glazed brown scabs. In a field of sawdust, wood shavings, and pencil nubs, a half-eaten sandwich lies in its crumbs, among moths, dying, dead, and dormant, and (to leave nothing out) the husks of a hundred flies.I am not allowed to disturb this disorder. It's an absolute rule. Also I am not allowed to bring it up for discussion, having done so once too often a few winters ago. I can still hear my voice, hinting how untidiness is a sympton of mental chaos, my voice, sounding like the voice of all women who think they can change the way things are.

The house is my domain, my responsibility, all of it except Stew's office. So I go around picking up after him, his skivvies, his balled-up tee shirts, the odd sock that shares the space under the bed with fur the dog has shed. Mother, forgive him, he knows not what he does.

Mind you I don't wash these clothes even when Stew's hamper runneth over, even though I was raised in the dark ages, trained to wash clothes for men. Here's how to bleach his shirts; here's how to starch his shirts; here's how to iron his shirts. Stew can do his own shirts. He did them before he met me. He can very well do them again. And he does so, willingly. We have that kind of modern relationship.

When my hamper runs over I get out the pickle buckets. I drop in the clothes, add some hot water, some soap. I let everything soak. A day or two later I slosh the clothes in the suds. I slosh them in rinse water, wring them, hang them dripping wet on the line. By now the clothes I am wearing are as wet as the clothes I have washed. I hang them on the line too. There they all hang for days, dripping, freezing, thawing, dripping again, freezing again. Sooner or later, like when Stew needs to use the line, I take in my frozen clothes, stiff as cardboard, hanging with icicles, nowhere near dry, nowhere near clean, the tee shirts pointed at the shoulders where clothespins pinched them to the line. Mother, we are not judged by our laundry.

Three times a week, Monday, Wednesday, and Friday, it is my chore to get the mail, even when those mornings dawn pitilessly cold and the snow is falling, flying, swirling thick. "You're not going to make *me* go out in that are you?"

"It's your chore."

See what I mean.

I never seem able to dress warmly enough even though I put on my entire 35-piece wool ensemble. I stomp stockinged feet into ski boots, drive mittened fists into the pockets of my parka. I put on that look of resignation I have learned to wear lately. Stew has become a hard-hearted man.

As I might have mentioned, must have mentioned, Stew has also become a driven man, a busy man. Even on glorious days, days easily lost and not seen again for weeks, he chooses to stay indoors, working, working! at his important desk, exchanging views with the supervisor of the Challis National Forest over one damn proposal after another. Thick reports spread before him, and old corre-spondences, drifts of paper, wadded-up typos. His coffee cup shakes, the table rattles every time he slaps the return. Clatter, thud, *ping*. Combing his furious beard with his fingers, locking his brows, he's just about to come up with a solution to it all.

"Er-um, want to go skiing?" I barge into Stew's work-in-progress. My asking is just a ritual now, just a formali-ty. I know his answer beforehand. I know how he will give his typewriter another whack, lift his eyes and peer at me over his glasses in that exaggerated way he has, then drop his eyes and twist his mouth in irritation at having his train of thought interrupted. "So how am I supposed to know you are having a train of thought?"

"Always assume that I am."

I smile, anxious to appear unhurt. Stew smiles, anxious to appear unhurtful. Whether from stress or aging, or both, he has lost his sense of fun. I am always disappointed in him for not wanting to ski and at myself for not wanting to ski without him. Stew and I are better together than we are apart, so I also stay indoors chained to my desk. Change has crept through me as well.

It wasn't always like this. When the boys lived here, desks and deadlines weren't part of our winters. There was more laughter then. Ah, them were the days.

Never ones to waste the sunshine, we gladly deferred our work to that time when storms would return. Every glorious day would find us crisscrossing the countryside on skinny skis, shush-shush-shushing through a world of monumental silence, a world of two mediums, snow and sky, white enamel and blue enamel. We never concerned ourselves with brute progress or miles per hour. We just moved our legs, one leg after another, rhythmically striding, poling, kicking, gliding, not flying exactly, but close to it. Through the long-shadowed aisles of aspens we went, through moments of brilliant sun and moments of cold blue shade. Objects advanced to meet us, moved past, receded behind us. Sometimes just for the hell of it, for the pure joy of being outdoors, we would hurtle shouts at the mountains, and the mountains would bounce around our shouts and fling them back, filling the canyon with joy. I did not know then that these were the best times of our lives.

Even Chad called this fun. But he never called this skiing, it wasn't worthy of the word. He could really ski. He could fly, and he did fly, even when the weather was all sideways and our ski trails were sidewalks of ice and everyone else stayed indoors where the yeasty smell of bread dough ballooning on the mantle and the spicy smell of chili bubbling lustily on the stove made us perpetually hungry. Through the spotting scope I watched Chad aboard his fat metal-edged skis, stomping sideways, stomping laboriously, to the top of his ski hill. Midway to the top he stopped and made a snowball to cool his brow (it must have been beating as hard as his heart). At the top he breathed deeply and taxied around, flapping his arm-wings, waiting to be cleared for take-off. He crouched, leaning far over his poles like ski racers do on TV. Then he sliced down the slope like a knife, a blur of red wool, showering snow spray at each little show-offy turn, totally incapable of falling. He glided to a stop, grinning, always grinning, as if a crowd was applauding his hot little moves. And not just his mom.

When the storms left our ski trails fluffy with six or eight inches of powder, before we could ski we had to pack the powder down with snowshoes. We have the older kind of snowshoes, the kind Indians still make with rawhide and wood, the kind you see crisscrossed over fireplace mantels.

And we did that, broke trail. It was both work and fun in equal measure. When we went to Corral Creek, one ridge over, we made a day of it, taking along chunks of elk meat for a barbecue. Up the hillside behind the house we went waddling web-footed, thrashing through the sagebrush, over the snow. Fifteen minutes and we topped the ridge. From here you can see Morgan Creek, Annie Roonie Creek, Van Horn Peak, Woods Peak, Sawmill Creek, our cabin—the eyesore that ought not to be there. You can see Corral Creek with its cabin and domestic pastures and barn propped by poles on the leaning-over side, and the broken-down corrals for which Corral Creek was named, this beautiful creek filled with fish, beavers, and ducks. All these creeks and peaks were named for humans and their

human-made structures. These names tell us nothing
about the places, how they look, what wild plants grow
there, what wild animals live there, what happened there
in the distant past or what was rumored to have happened
there.

What happened on Corral Creek in the near past,
about eight years ago, was that some people from Texas
rented the old log cabin, a young couple with two toddlers.
One day, prodded by curiosity and not much else, Stew and
I went over to meet them, snowshoed the two miles separating our cabin from theirs. It was obvious that over the
summer our new neighbors had gone to a lot of work making the old cabin livable, trapping the mice and woodrats,
or most of them, stuffing plaster into the wall gaps, or the
worse of them. They had paneled the living room walls and
curtained the kitchen windows. He had patched the roof of
the barn and cranked up its leaning-over side so it was
level, or level enough anyway, for it was here he would
keep the hay for his horses. With orange bailing twine he
fixed two of the corrals to keep in his milk cow and beef
cow, and a third corral to keep out the deer, for it was here
she would plant her vegetable garden.

After our first visit there came a second visit and a
third. Almost weekly that winter we snowshoed over to the
cabin on Corral Creek. We did this even though we shared
no interest with these people other than gardening and no
values at all, they being the kind of people whose net value
of things is calculated in food and dollars, whose relationship with wildlife is unloving, businesslike, and brutal.
Being so young, they knew just about everything homesteaders need to know, how to fence, how to plow, how to
trap beavers, bobcats, and fox, how to butcher, how to raise
crops, chickens, horses, cows, pigs, and kids. They told us
all this not so much to impress us but to reassure themselves.

The next winter, having grown to know them better, having grown to like them less, we visited them less but often enough to know that sheer human cussedness was getting them by. Her harvest of corn, squash, and beans was about as bountiful as you might expect here in USDA Zone Two. With his pastures hock-deep in snow he was having to feed his livestock store-bought hay, something he could ill afford, the market for furs being so poor and the fur-bearers all but trapped out the winter before.

It was not nature that kicked the teeth out of their homesteading dream. It was their landlord. They had wanted to buy a place of their own, their own piece of paradise, low monthly payments, nothing down. So they went to her, would she sell them the back pasture on Corral Creek? No she would not. She would not sell the back pasture or any pasture, to them or to anyone else, under any conditions, ever, end of discussion. This put them in a snit. At some point they must have decided that the pastures in Texas were just as green as the pastures in central Idaho, if not greener. Within a matter of weeks they sold what they had to, their horses and cows. They packed up their traps, their babies and pigs, their chickens and chicken hawk guns, and without as much as a good-bye they went back to Texas. Stew and I felt bad that we didn't feel bad enough.

The beavers, bobcats, and fox staged a comeback in celebration of their leaving. When the back pasture grew back the elk came back. When the corrals fell down the deer harvested the volunteer lettuce and beets. When the plaster fell out the mice and the woodrats moved in, in greater numbers than before, and two starlings flew in with bugs clamped in their beaks. Now it's hard to believe that eight years ago anybody lived there at all.

Another part of that winter, and all those winters that

were, was our Churchwell School for Boys, a less than joyful series of hour-long classes designed to duplicate the
tried and true ways of the little red schoolhouse. Stew
caged the boys in the schoolroom, first Roy, then Chad, Roy
being a grade higher than Chad. With textbooks they were
taught math. They were taught history and geography
with textbooks and forced memorization and pop quizzes
and all those dirty tricks teachers use to get kids to
remember dates and presidents and state capitols, useless
facts that kids forget as soon as summer comes, knowledge
they don't need to know.

Meanwhile in the living room I taught whomever Stew
wasn't teaching. I taught science, some of which I still
don't fully comprehend. I taught English, and as the learn-
ers learned, I learned, or rather I relearned, all the pitfalls
of punctuation and just how treacherous English spellings
are. Air, heir, e'er, ere all sound the same.

As you can probably see, as I can definitely see, our
Churchwell School for Boys embodied much of what is
wrong with public schools. Without ever considering the
alternatives, and there were plenty of alternatives, Stew
and I brought into our home the institutional regimenta-
tion of public schools, we were that regimented ourselves,
that unsure of ourselves, that butt-dumb. That's the crying
shame of it. We wasted the boys' time and energy. We
would have wasted their inherent love of learning had we
not managed to get some things right.

For one thing, Stew taught the boys only basic math
since he could see, right off, they were not wonders with
numbers. For another thing, I gave them dictionaries (and
hoped for the best) when I could see they found no redeem-
ing meaning in spelling lists. Best of all, with our two stu-
dents-two teachers advantage, Stew and I were able to get
through the textbooks by March, at the latest, after which
time we taught the boys what they wanted to learn. And

wonder of wonders. After March they still wanted to learn and we still wanted to teach.

Chad's interests lay inside the workshed where Stew gave hands-on instruction in small engine repair, leather making, and basic guitar. Basic woodshop turned piles of scrap lumber into bluebird boxes, twelve of them. Every spring bluebirds nest in the box Stew made. House wrens nest in the boxes Chad made, and tree swallows, chickadees, and chipmunks.

But Chad's interests didn't include art in any form. His hurried scribbles and furrowed brow made an unmistakable statement early on. So with Chad we never went beyond coloring books even as we plied Roy with sketch pads, pen and ink, oil paints and water colors, colored chalks and colored pencils. Like all proud parents we marveled at Roy's talent. Let me marvel further. It is not so farfetched to believe that Roy has enough talent, enough dedication, to make art his life's work.

As I hope is obvious by now, these boys, these brothers, their interests, their talents were worlds apart. Where Roy collected insects, mounted them, labeled them, studied them, Chad squashed them. Where Roy clipped wild plants, pressed them, labeled them, studied them, Chad tore them up by the roots and brought them home to me in fragrant strangled bouquets (Chad also brought me rusty bear traps, elk's jaws, wasp nests, and rocks, lots and lots of rocks).

What the boys did have in common was their love for reading. They became hopelessly hooked on books. Maybe it was because they weren't required to do book reports. More likely it was because a television wasn't handy. In other words they had nothing else to do but read.

Thanks to the Challis library, the Hub, yard sales, and friends, especially friends, we were able to feed the boys' appetite for books, their appetite for books having grown bigger than their appetite for food. Being the perfect child Roy liked to read what Stew and I liked to read, that is, anything and everything having to do with nature. Being a slightly less than perfect child Chad liked to read–no, he devoured–anything and everything having to do with guns, grudges, and mayhem in the old West.

What we read aloud in the evenings after dinner was of my choosing, I being the teacher of English lit, I being a lover of good books, of books filled with old-fashioned values like how to live right, how to be brave, honest, and loving, wonderful books like *The Yearling*, *Old Yeller*, *The Incredible Journey*, *The Education of Little Tree*, *Where the Sidewalk Ends*, *Where the Red Fern Grows*, and *Little House on the Prairie*.

Most of the time before bedtime was given over to reading, Stew and I sitting on the couch, the boys on the rug at our feet, Roy stretching his long lean frame to full length, reading to us in a monotone while he tried to decide what, if anything, it all meant. Chad, typical Chad, read folded up into himself, interrupting himself with questions and comments, getting ahead of himself, smiling to himself, unsmiling, smiling again, rolling his eyes, shaking his head, his voice packed with emotions, edged with tears, then laughter, then huge laughter with a couple of snorts thrown in.

For both boys, but to a greater extent for Roy, the best classroom by far was the outdoors where learning was ongoing and related directly to life. Lying in their sleeping bags beneath a sky full of stars, deep stars, and stars deeper still, they got pretty strong clues about the character of infinity. Beside the lakes, when fish were slow to bite, they waded in the shallows, turning over rocks, searching for the living things all kids are prone to search for. Field guides gave names to the caddisfly larvae they watched crawling across the lake bottoms, encased in portable tubes of glued-together sand.

When elk hunting with Stew how could a kid not notice the geology going on around him, how the very outcrops they had to skirt were folded, fractured, tilted, and stacked. Field dressing an elk doubled as an anatomy lesson, although it was never called that in so many words. Stew simply pulled from the cavity all the organs packed tight and moist, cleaned them up as best he could, and handed them to the boys. "That's the heart. That's the liver. Those are the kidneys."

Of course, there were those who argued that schooling the boys at home, home being Sawmill Creek, was not in the boys' best interest. These critics–the school board, the superintendent, the grandmas, even friends–felt that isolation was depriving the boys of the social contact so essential to education. Our response was one of denial. Stew and I saw it all right, the sense of it, the nonsense of it, but we didn't want to believe it even as isolation was beginning to cripple Chad emotionally, this lonesome teenager Chad. We saw it most convincingly when our friends came for rare visits on summer weekends. Hours before they were due to arrive Chad lay in wait at the gate, anxious and fearful they might not come at all. When they did arrive they were greeted as if they had found their way across the frozen Arctic. When it came time for them to go, past the time for them to go, he held them still, taking them happily up the canyon one last time, showing them, with the pride of an owner, with sweeping waves of his hand, where the moose stood one spring, where the bear chased Mom, trying to distract them, hoping they might forget to go at all. But they always left and after they left Chad sulked. During these monstrous marathons of sulking he cursed his life, cursed his isolation, cursed anything else he could think of.

So there you have it. We did our best but the boys left home anyway, before it was time. I'm not saying whether this was good or bad, only that they left home and life went on, not as usual, but life went on.

For the fifth time in as many years Christmas comes to Chad in care of Bird City and to Roy in care of Challis. It comes to Sawmill Canyon so peacefully you wonder if it came at all. Stew and I are never the ones to cling blindly to holiday traditions. After the boys left we decided to just say no to it all, to the festoonery, to counting down the shopping days, to mail-ordering gifts, to sending cards, to sacrificing a living tree, to listening to canned Christmas carols surging and fading from our portable radio. We don't miss any of it. Not even a little bit.

With no effort on our part Sawmill Canyon looks as Christmasy as a greeting card, as the December page of a calendar, as a paperweight full of flying snow. There in the snow stands our cabin, chimney smoke upcurling, golden lamplight gleaming, spilling out the windows and over the snowdrifts curled around. There are acres of snow-flocked firs trimmed with real cones and real icicles. There's the mailbox full of the small joys that come in red handwritten envelopes. Peace on Earth. There are larger joys wrapped in boxes so big I have to ski them home strapped to my backpack. You see, our friends and families believe, quite mistakenly, that Christmas on Sawmill Creek, especially without the boys, is as bleak as Christmas on the moon.

Why gifts come matters to us very little. With childlike dispatch we rip into everything early on Christmas Eve, if we can wait even that long. There are boxes of dried fruit and cuddly pajamas and wonderful books hot off the press. In a box so big I have to sled it home, my mother sends grapefruits from her garden and roses wrapped in wet paper towels, still red and fragrant after their thousand-mile trip. At the bottom of her box, cradled in tissue paper, are new toothbrushes and hand lotions and bottles of vitamin C. My mother, being my mother, still likes to mother me, tenderly, dependably, even in my old age.

In a no-fuss atmosphere Stew and I sit down to our tribal feast, both of us at one end of the dinner table, a table I have arranged with the red slab candles my mother sent and the fragrant fir boughs I collected while festively freezing my buns off. Stew does the dinner, a sumptuous meal with lovely parslied potatoes, baby carrots, and small sweet onions, everything delicately browned in roasting juices, and the elk roast done medium rare, done per-fecto . . . well, it makes me cry just to think about it.

New Years Eve is as lively as Christmas Eve. Stew does the complete dinner again if he feels like it or if he doesn't he makes up a plate of sandwiches. In either case our domestic evening of eating in is followed by a little mild well-modulated stimulation, no excitement, no pretending a joyful delirium. No balloons. No stupid hats. No drunken revelry. With Stew's home-brew we toast, *tink*, clinking our glasses together. Here's to our continued partnership. Here's to our continued unemployment. Here's to our splendid isolation. We smack our lips. *Glug-glug-glug*. That's as wild as it gets.

We don't count down the old year's clock, another break with tradition that bothers us not a whit. While the rest of America makes merry, we bed down at eight o'clock, like we always do, New Years Eve being just like any other winter eve on Sawmill Creek. Dressed in our inelegant evening apparel–long johns and jammies–we read for an hour, or when reading is not the thing, we let ourselves be bored sleepy by radio talk shows, our laps full of yarn and leather. Tell us, folks, what do you think of this? What do you think of that? Tell us how you are going to welcome in the new year, another year, another dreary, weary year. On the hour, on the half, and when it breaks, the world news, the weeping shrieking news, comes clawing its way through the static, into our living room lit like a bright planet in the black void of never-ending space. Bloody uprisings and bloody put-downs. Cold wars and hot little battles. Airplane crashes, AIDS, mutant viruses. Shootings in the work place. Hey, let's be careful out there.

It's January – all month. It's colder, much colder, much too cold. The trail to the mailbox is glassy with cold, with ice, dazzling, blinding, maddening white. I hop-step it into long johns. I put on one, two, three of everything I own: pants, shirts, sweaters, socks, wool caps, boot liners, boots, gaiters, earmuffs, vest, wrap-around scarf, left mitten, right mitten . . . right mitten . . . where is that mitten? It must be . . . somewhere . . . where?

Bundled in all these clothes I am an unrecognizable creature. I can hardly bend over much less perform the full-body contortions needed to strap on snowshoes. On the positive side, most of what I wear is made of cotton and wool. Should I be buried in an avalanche I can eat these clothes to stay alive. Needless to say, I am as reluctant as ever to go forth into the Great White Death. Stew finds this a form of weakness. "Cold make you feel *alive!*"

Cold *kills!* At the very least I could lose fingers, ear-lobs, a piece of my nose. I hunch my shoulders up around my ears, pull my snowcap over my eyebrows. Only my eyes are uncovered. My breath is a cloud of steam. One mile down. Turn around. One mile back.

Rifling through the mail, looking for something that never seems to come, I see most of it is for Stew. The rest goes into the stove unopened (my ten million dollar prize will be sent to someone else). Into the stove go the magazine samples that assault my nose with perfume and gift catalogs full of things I never knew I needed. Into the stove go form letters from well-meaning groups needing money to save the seals, the starving children in Ethiopia, the starving children in Cambodia, the rain forests, the spotted owl, the frogs – lost causes Stew can do nothing about. Gee, I wonder where they got our address.

Garbage in, garbage out. If we didn't cremate all this junkmail we'd be buried alive before we could get to the dump. As it is, most winters, what we can't burn or compost or recycle fits nicely into four plastic trash bags. That's six months' worth of trash in just four trash bags. I say this as if it were our life's greatest achievement which indeed it just might be.

These four trash bags are stored handily in our travel trailer, I hesitate to call it a dumpster, it is also our emergency housing should the cabin burn down one winter in spite of our precautions. Blocked by miles of drifted snow the Challis Volunteer Fire Department could not respond even if we could contact them which of course we can't. Since we wouldn't be able to save everything, we would probably try to save nothing but our sorry selves. I have figured out how we will to do that. I have stocked the trailer with clothes, sleeping bags, and enough food and propane for two weeks. Should the cabin burn down during a storm when we can't go for help (where we would go for help I haven't got figured out yet), time will pass pleasantly enough with books and board games. Naturally Stew and I will do a lot of serious talking, like where in the hell do we go from here. Stew doesn't feel that building another cabin is such a big deal. Having built one he is perfectly capable of building another. But the thing of it is, well, I don't really know the complete thing of it, but I don't think I have another cabin in *me*.

"So what about medical emergencies? What if you break your leg? Then what'll you do?" My mother would sleep better if I could reach out and touch someone at the Custer County Sheriff's Office, if not by phone, then by something like Ship-to-Shore or Sawmill-to-Ski-Patrol or Space-Station-to-Ground-Control. So what'll I do if I break my leg? Well . . . um . . . I'm thinking, I'm thinking. Probably Stew could sled me down the driveway and down Morgan Creek Road to where it runs out of snow. Then he could hitchhike me piggybacked to the first-aid station where the Life Flight helicopter would fly me to whatever hospital will take us uninsured hippies. In other words I don't know what we will do but we certainly can't hibernate all winter. Over and out.

That Stew and I have wintered without mishap all these years is scarcely accidental. To a large extent medical emergencies are as preventable as house fires (the act of saying that convinces me it is so). It's always a good idea to be careful when working around hot grease. Watch out that you don't cut yourself on sharp knives. Don't start the chainsaw in winter. Don't forget your mittens. Don't fall.

It's not that my mother's fears have no merit mind you. But they are not the point here, the point being that nature sets the conditions by which Stew and I live and we must accept those conditions or give up living here entirely. That's just the way it goes.

I never know when the end of January ends and the beginning of February begins. The landscape hasn't changed noticeably since December. The trees are stark and without promise, the sky a cold, impersonal blue. There are days I would give anything to see a butterfly go by, even just part of a butterfly, I get so awfully sick of the frozen scene at the windows. My mind has frozen. Time has frozen, it goes so slowly, it has no value, there is so much of it. I flip the calendar and begin marking time with a felt-tip pen, x-ing out each day as each day is over and done. But I no sooner get one day done then here comes another day, or is it the same day come again, it's hard to tell, all the days are just units of time: time to get up, time for breakfast, time for lunch, time for dinner, then bed, then wake up it's morning and time to do it all again. And in the night my dreams are the days all over again, the same, the same, there is nothing else to tell. My journal entries, when I find the ambition to write, deteriorate into dashed-off scrawls. "Got up. Had oatmeal. Wrote in my journal."

Did I really choose this life? Or was I condemned to it? I can't get interested in anything, including food. I take my fork and knife to whatever is put upon my plate and chew it with bovine indifference, or rather, I shift it around in my mouth, trying to find one sound molar to grind it on, most of my teeth are root-sprung. Sometimes it's just easier to eat dinner standing up, at the sink, out of the pan. Or is this lunch? Have I had lunch yet? It's definitely too much trouble to make any kind of decision, even a simple decision. Should I do the dishes or not do the dishes? Should I sweep or not sweep or sort of sweep?

Waiting for winter to end becomes my obsession. Slapping slippers back and forth across the floor, stirring up little storms of discontent, I talk back to the radio, I fill the house with my grievances, most of which have to do with the weather, the lousy weather, I lay it all on Stew who never complains. I don't believe he is capable of it. That is not his outlet. "For one month you are bored," he says. "The rest of the year you are doing what you want. That's a damn sight better than the world average."

I write, "Dear Mother, Dear God, Help me I'm dying. These days, these many days—oh never mind!" Tear up the letter.

I try to draw spiritual nourishment from my mother's letters, postmarked Sunshine Villas, Planet Palm Springs.

I rip into them, at the mailbox, in a snowstorm. Snapshots spill out the envelopes, of little family doings, chatty little dinners out. There's a Christmas tree in one picture. There are balloons and stupid hats in another. There's my entire family beside the cool blue swimming pool, everyone radiating vitality, glowing under their terrific tennis tans, everyone looking younger than I remembered, how I miss them all. Their merry eyes look out at me as if to say that somewhere at least there is sunshine, there is heat, there is happiness. I feel very far away from them in more ways than just miles. I say "them" in wistful tones, meaning, people. I want to live a real life, like other people, eat pepperoni pizzas, watch stupid sitcoms, gossip across phone lines, merge with the freeway rush, attend staff meetings, stand in grocery store lines at 11 p.m.

Just about the time I fall into something precariously close to ruin, March comes along and opens a breathing hole for my spirit. Something is definitely going on around here. It's neither spring nor winter nor anything else you could specify. The air just smells differently, as if it were about to change—coming soon to a neighborhood near you: THE BIG THAW. Unable to contain myself, I do a backward flip, or the middle-aged equivalent of such.

Winter never vanishes mysteriously overnight, but sometime around mid-March spring becomes imaginable. With the sun high and fierce, the thick swirling snow cannot swallow all the light. Icicles drip. The roof steams. Great slabs of snow break off the roof, come hissing off the metal, crashing down to the ground. The sun burns the snow on the trails, making them so soft and mushy my skis grow platforms inches thick.

Sawmill is not yet the paradise of fecundity it will become in June but there is life in late March. Witness the chains of mouse prints, broken here by the long looping line of a weasel, broken there by the wing fan of an owl.

Judging by Cujo's behavior, the coyote bitches have gone into estrus, drenching the trails with perfume, well, perfume from a canine perspective, their scents saying in essence, "Hey, Cujo, I am ready to mate. To find me, follow your nose." Cujo sniffs the trails, sniffs the snow where they sat, sniffs even their shadows.

For reasons I can't imagine, snowfleas are out, hopping around, small as pinpoints, and tiny long-legged spiders stalking them in slow-motion pursuit. There are butterflies—butterflies!—dozens of tortoiseshells floating around, bright as flowers, more welcome than flowers, and mourning cloaks darker than tree bark, standing stark against the snow, their wings so tattered, so weak, it's a wonder they still work. As the sap begins to flow in the aspens so my blood begins to flow with energy, ambition, and the kind of restlessness that drives the birds back from wherever they flew off to in the fall. Welcome to my world.

11
Speaking of Spring

Ere long, not only on these banks, but on every hill and plain and in every hollow, the frost comes out of the ground like a dormant quadruped from its burrow, and seeks the sea with music, or migrates to other climes in clouds. Thaw with his gentle persuasion is more powerful than Thor with his hammer. The one melts, the other but breaks in pieces.
–Henry David Thoreau

Spring cannot just come but it must be heralded by signs, attended by visible evidence that the land is in molt. After months of silently falling snow I hear the first soft raindrops pinging the greenhouse roof, pattering in that delightful way that makes you feel such a pleasant sense of shelter, under cover, warm and dry. There are bud bumps on the twiggy winter willows and shoots of green to indicate hope. On the south-facing hillsides, bluebells are shoving the dirt aside. Where rocks have melted the meadows in spots, buttercups make a brave display of waxy blooms.

The hardy advanced guard of migrants, having found their way back, their hormones humming, wing through the soft blue air of April. I never ignore the return of my birds. I drop everything, dishes in the sink, floor half mopped, knitting needles mid-row, whatever I am doing I lay it aside. Radiant with joy I attend to their arrival.

The trick here is to design an excuse to cover two or three hours away from home. "First I'm getting the mail, then I'm getting mushrooms." I'm really getting to know the birds better, what on earth else should I be doing. The wonderful newness of the birds has not worn off yet as it should have. I still travel through spring fairly awed. I walk languorously through it, like the red-tailed hawks circling the hillside, hanging in the air for a few moments of meditation.

Soon or not so soon I am home. I find Stew cloistered in his office, the door closed against me, he means nothing rude. A babble of environmental buzzwords slip through the cracks. With the superiority of an outdoors person joining a sedentary friend, I go barging into his work-in-progress, interrupting his train of thought, tracking his floor with mud. "Back already? Is it that late?"

"Want to know what I saw?"

"Not now. I'm busy. Everything's got to be in the mail by yesterday."

"Alright, I'll tell you." And dutifly I tell him about the birds, all about the birds if he lets me or only a little something about the birds if he doesn't, as if just naturally he would care about a vireo or would even know what a vireo was. Stew listens to me and I listen to me. I glance at him now and then for some sign of interest, encouragement, appreciation, and when nothing comes, when I see how his eyes narrow with impatience, his lips curl into his mouth, I lose the thread of my story, lose all interest in telling it. Yet for some inexplicable reason I chirp on and on, a headlong, all or nothing, rush. I straighten papers on his desk, line up files and pencils, trying to shut myself up. My voice comes to a stumbling halt. There is silence. More silence, a period of thoughtful review. I wait. So does he. But I wait longer. Something more needs to be said but I can't think what it is.

"So, you had a good walk, then." Stew says this weari-
ly, as if to a tiresome child. I have nothing to say to this,
absolutely nothing to say. And perhaps that's just as well.

To unwind from a long hard day of simple pleasures,
after dinner I try the porch for relaxation, lowering myself
into my willow chair as if it were a hot bath, luxuriating in
the peace, the silence, the extreme remoteness from that
other world, that noisy man-made world. "Come out, come
out," I call to Stew. "Come out and hear the owls." Stew
comes out. He hears the owls. "Listen to the ruffed grouse."
He listens to the ruffed grouse. *Thrump thrump-thrump-
thrump-thrump-p-p-p-p-p*. We listen to the nighthawks
booming, diving, their fringed mouths spread wide for
insects. We let the evening come over us, drawing us closer together.

Like any old country couple (if this is old age it's not so
awful), side-by-side we sit, the song of the hermit thrush
spiraling through our souls, our eyes gazing into the west,
watching the sunset outdo the splendor of the dawn,
watching the dusk darken by indistinguishable degrees
the vast sweeps of lupines even as their perfume fills the
canyon to the brim. Van Horn Peak, three miles distant,
keeps its distance, casts no shadow upon our porch.

There's enough light left to see the deer migrating
back from their riverside haystacks, and the elk, mangy as
junkyard dogs, their ribs showing, their coats in molted
tatters. Pronghorns are our favorite fauna. Up the driveway they come, in that hesitant way they have, half afraid,
half curious. The leader, a mature buck, stops at the gate,
waiting for his herd to pass through. He butts a reluctant
yearling, pursues a panicky doe, heading her off like a
good cutting horse at a rodeo. Then the herd is through the
gate and dashing over the hillsides, one flowing unit,

white flags waving until they are out of sight, swallowed up, every one, by distance and the dark.

Stew pops open a second brew, drinks from it with a loud smacking of lips, a savage thirst to quench. He uncases his guitar, his six-string, and lifts it from its fleece-lined cradle. He toys with the strings, experiments with the chords. Feet propped on the railing, he breaks into song, heaves himself into song, a bogus cowboy twang. He makes music, not great music but his music, coming close enough to the right notes and the right words, his voice so pleasant I am tempted to believe anything he sings. I want a few more minutes outside. Just a few more minutes.

It's wonderful, that's what it is, these perfumed evenings. Stew and I. Box seats. Ringside. I want to live out my old age right here in this willow chair, wrapped in a grandmother's quilt, scanning the west for whatever it is I am meant to see. I am loathed to return to civilization, such as it is in Challis. On the other hand, Stew's enthusiasm is unbearable. He has phone calls to make, reports to photocopy, a meeting in town, where he will take his place among a crowd of Wild West hats and a handful of environmentalists, most of them rascally outsiders. He tells me the trailer smells of garbage, like something died in there. The laundry is spilling out the hampers and across the floor. He needs gaskets for the ram pump and building materials for the summer projects I have planned. He says it's just time to go out, meaning it, meaning no more discussing it.

We turn the house upside down in preparation. Since Stew wants to go out before it's time to go out, he spends several days beforehand hacking down snowdrifts in the driveway. I think he enjoys this. He likes fighting with the driveway, likes defeating it.

He installs the truck battery, cleans and connects the terminals. He dumps the mouse nests out of the housing for the air cleaner. He checks all the fluid levels. He turns over the key. Will the truck-the-truck-the-truck-st-st-st-st-st-start? I never want it to but it starts. While the engine chuffs away, dirty brown smoke puffing out the exhaust pipe, Stew puts on the tire chains. We are ready. Almost.

For these meetings Stew must look his best, well-dressed, well-barbered. I cut his hair, or rather I sculpt it, it's so fine, more like bird feathers than hair. He is growing lots of forehead.

With a hand mirror propped against the sugar bowl on the dinner table, Stew trims his thick curly sideburns growing into his wild-grown beard. He scrubs dried oatmeal out of this gray-shot bush of a beard, washes it, trims it down to an inch, inch and a half, shaves it clean under his lower lip, except for a little tuft smack in the middle. He trims his mustache artistically above the upper lip and where it has crept into his mouth, even though he nibbled on it all winter. He swaths his baldness in a brightly colored bandana, the hippie headscarf he has decided will be his hallmark. He checks himself out in the bathroom mirror, then again, several more times, inspecting his face. Admiring is a better word.

Like a snake sheds its old skin, Stew sheds his long johns and fuzzball wool socks. There they are, his white fuzzy legs, his bald white knees, his feet, bare, boncy, puckered like they had been long submerged in water. After showering he shimmies into his go-to-town jeans. He pulls on his favorite tee shirt: NO MOOS IS GOOD NEWS (he really means it). With his boots spit-shined to a glow, he is ready. We are ready. Almost.

"Are you really going to town looking like that? Wearing that? That? People will point." I know perfectly well what I look like and I am not pleased. It's been a long winter, you understand. I try to put myself to rights, put my hair in some kind of order, furiously try to brush it into submission. I catch sight of myself in the mirror. My hair looks worse brushed. I don't want to inspect that face any closer. I slip into something light and cottony, something casual. Having inherited my mother's distaste for glamour, I don't really have a dress-up wardrobe. Formal attire suits me poorly, just as poorly as attending formal functions: meetings, weddings, funerals, banquets. I will buy a dress as soon as I figure out what I need one for.

"Are you ready? Are you ready? Are you hanging on the edge of your seat?" Stew is as excited as a child at Christmas. He starts the truck for the wild ride ahead. He hunches over the steering wheel, clutching it in a white-knuckled grip. I sit strapped into the passenger seat, my hands involuntarily clenched, forming fists on either side of me. Nervous? Me? Stew rams the gearshift into first, reverse, first, rocking the truck forward, backward, forward, and free. We leave a brown rectangle in our wake.

Stew handles the truck like a stock-car racer, gassing it here, breaking it there, playing with the sticks on the floor, shifting hard. I close my eyes as down the driveway we go sliding, wheel-spinning, granny gear screaming, chains crunching, chunking, slapping the fenders, mud and snow roostertailing out the back. I don't think we ever go straight to our direction of travel. Around one corner and Stew corrects a bit too much, loses it to the other side. Around another corner and through the opened window a willow branch slaps me *thwack*! in the face. Then something . . . eek! a mouse, pops its head out the hole in the shifter boot, runs over my feet. Things start popping out the defrost vents on the dashboard. Spitballs! Of course. Happens every year. Same old story. Mouse chews spare roll of toilet paper in glove compartment. Mouse makes nest in engine. Two words come to mind. Oh dear. Stew's scarf, mustache, and beard are flecked with toilet paper, his shoulders and shirt front–all his good grooming spoiled. But what is important here is that we made it to Morgan Creek Road. From here it's smooth sailing. From winter we are free.

It occurs to me that this is as good a place as any to end my book, this story to which I know the beginning but whose ending I am still trying to imagine. But are books ever finished? I think not. Writers just get tired of writing. I know. I have been working on *Cabin* for ten years, off and on, putting it aside, returning to it, rewriting it, quitting it, starting something else, coming back to it (during this time I twice decided to give it up and once decided to give up writing entirely). The  problem is, my story has no natural ending because our life on Sawmill Creek hasn't ended. It keeps recycling in a pattern of constant recurrences, as the seasons keep recycling forever, on and on. I can't see anything changing until Stew and I are carried off into the hereafter (it happens!) Nevertheless, I must end it, publish it, so my mother will stop nagging me to write a book. David Henry had all the best lines, he may as well have the last:

I will take another walk to the Cliff, another row on the river, another skate on the meadow, be out in the first snow, and associate with the winter birds. Here I am at home. In the bare and bleached crust of the earth I recognize my friend.

The End

Other Caxton Books about Idaho

River Tales of Idaho
by Darcy Williamson
ISBN 0-87004-378-1 342 pages paper $17.95

Southern Idaho Ghost Towns
by Wayne Sparling
ISBN 0-87004-229-7 135 pages paper $12.95

Gem Minerals of Idaho
by John A. Beckwith
ISBN 0-87004-228-9 129 pages paper $9.95

Tiger on the Road
The Life of Vardis Fisher
by Tim Woodword
ISBN 0-87004-333-1 269 pages paper $14.95
ISBN 0-87004-338-2 cloth $19.95

For a free catalog of Caxton books write to:

The CAXTON PRINTERS, Ltd.
Publishing Department
312 Main Street
Caldwell, ID 83605

or

Visit our Internet Website:

www.caxtonprinters.com